THE BATSFORD GUIDE TO
THE INDUSTRIAL ARCHAEOLOGY OF THE BRITISH ISLES
General Editor : Keith Falconer

South-East England

Frontispiece Argos Hill post mill, near Rotherfield in East Sussex

The Batsford Guide to the Industrial Archaeology of

South-East England

KENT   SURREY   EAST SUSSEX   WEST SUSSEX

A.J. HASELFOOT

B.T. Batsford Ltd · *London*

First published 1978
© A.J. Haselfoot 1978

ISBN 0 7134 1561 4 (Hardback)
      0 7134 1562 2 (Paperback)

Filmset by Servis Filmsetting Ltd, Manchester
Printed in Great Britain by
Butler & Tanner Ltd, Frome
for the publishers
B.T. Batsford Ltd
4 Fitzhardinge Street, London W1H 0AH

Foreword

Our knowledge, and hence appreciation, of our industrial heritage is, as yet, very inadequate, despite increasing interest in industrial archaeology in the last two decades. This is especially true of an area such as the South-East which has hitherto not received any comprehensive review of the remains of its industrial past. So many of the crucial processes of industrialization were pioneered in this country and brought about a revolution which has profoundly influenced the foundation and development of all industrialized societies. Its relics are thus monuments of the greatest relevance to our present society. Also of importance and even more vulnerable are the reminders of relatively modern industrial developments only recently made obsolete. These are being erased in a more thorough and systematic fashion, be it in the name of industrial rationalization, urban renewal or land reclamation – even if their preservation is impossible, their passing must be noted and at least recorded.

The pre-eminent place Britain holds in the foundation and continuing development of industrial archaeology is internationally acknowledged. There has been an impressive accumulation of material relating to industrial monuments ever since the phrase 'industrial archaeology' gained general acceptance in the late 1950s. In 1963 Rex Wailes, the noted authority on windmills, was appointed as consultant to the National Survey of Industrial Monuments. This Survey, under the joint aegis of the Council for British Archaeology and the Ministry of Public Buildings and Works sought to identify those industrial sites which merited statutory protection. On Wailes' retirement in 1971 the Survey was based at the University of Bath with a full time Survey Officer and its work continues apace now funded entirely by the Department of the Environment. Further evidence of the growing interest in industrial archaeology is provided by the staggering increase in the number of industrial museums ranging from large company and regional open air museums such as Wheal Martyn China Clay Museum in Cornwall, and Beamish North of England Open Air Museum, to single monument sites preserved by small voluntary trusts. A recent publication lists more than 150 industrial museums and monuments open to the public, most of which have been established in the last two decades. This trend is well represented in the South-East with examples ranging from the magnificent beam engines of Goldstone Pumping Station, Hove, now the focus of an ambitious engineerium, and Weald and Downland Open Air Museum, Singleton, with its charcoal makers' camp, donkey wheel pump and forge, to the scant remains of the once important Kentish gunpowder industry preserved by local enthusiasts at Chart Mills, Faversham.

The Batsford series, of which this is the second English volume, is the first major national series to concentrate on sites themselves as a prime source of evidence of this crucial phase of the nation's development. The Batsford series grew out of informal discussions between Neil Cossons, Director of the Ironbridge Gorge Museum and President of the Association for Industrial Archaeology,

Peter Kemmis Betty, Managing Director of Batsford, and myself. It comprehensively covers mainland Britain with two volumes each on Scotland and Wales, and thirteen volumes on England. These volumes systematically list most of those sites where complete or substantial remains can be seen. They will include some 20,000 sites and will thus constitute by far the most comprehensive survey ever attempted in this field. The four modern counties, which comprise this volume, contain a wide variety of types of industrial monuments. Historically the three maritime counties have shared a role of being the gateway to the continent, their ports being guarded by naval dockyards and military establishments and served by prestigious turnpike, and later rail, links to the capital. More recently their additional role as pleasure resorts led to the construction of an exceptional collection of elegant cast-iron piers such as those at Brighton and Eastbourne. The railway monuments range from the rather inconspicuous remains of the Canterbury and Whitstable railway of 1830 with the blocked portals of the oldest passenger railway tunnel in the country to the magnificent viaducts and tunnels of the Brighton and Dover lines.

The economies of Kent and Surrey have long been dominated by the proximity of London both as a market and as administrative and military capital of the kingdom. The majority of their industrial monuments reflect this dependence with agricultural based industries such as hop processing, milling and brewing being most prominent. The counties of Sussex, on the other hand, share a notable industrial tradition of iron manufacture but, although the pages of the Bulletin of the Wealden Iron Research Group record many iron working sites from Roman date onwards, there are few physical remains left above ground, other than hammer ponds, to witness the past importance of this industry. The incidental examples of its products such as the cast-iron tombstones at Wadhurst are more evident than the scant remains of the sites themselves such as Ashburnham furnace.

John Haselfoot, the author of the present volume, is a retired engineer and has long been a member of the Wind and Watermill section of the Society for the Protection of Ancient Buildings. He is general secretary of the Sussex Industrial Archaeology Society and, besides coordinating the county survey for the National Survey of Industrial Monuments, he has been prominent in the restoration of Bateman's watermill and Coultershaw water pump. In the last three years he has diligently visited almost all the sites mentioned in the gazetteer and it is to be hoped that such an example will stimulate intensive local surveys and research in these hitherto neglected areas.

Keith Falconer
National Survey of Industrial Monuments
November 1977

Contents

Acknowledgements

In the preparation of this book I have received help from many people: A.G. Allnutt, W.R. Beswick, F.W. Gregory and E.J. Upton; my fellow members of the Sussex Industrial Archaeology Society; F.E. Haveron of the Industrial Archaeology Section of the Surrey Archaeological Society; Mr and Mrs R.J. Spain of the Kent Archaeological Society; M. Forwood of the East Kent Mills Group; A. Percival of the Faversham Society; P.A. Daniell of the British Waterways Board and A.L. Hassell of the National Coal Board, Dover. I am also most grateful to the many people who have allowed me to inspect mills, engines and other items on their property and to D. Pratt for permission to reproduce two photographs of the lock and footbridge at Dartford. In compiling the gazetteer I have made much use of *Sussex Industrial Archaeology – A Field Guide* by J. Hoare and E.J. Upton, *The Windmills of Kent* by J. West, *Cliff Railways* by G. Body and R.L. Eastleigh, *Surrey Industrial Archaeology* by G.A. Payne, *The Watermills of Kent* by C.E. Bennett, *Forgotten Railways – South-East England* by H.P. White and a number of papers by John and Sue Farrant – my grateful thanks to these authors and the authors of many other publications I have consulted. I cannot pretend to have covered every single item of industrial archaeological interest in South-East England and I shall be most grateful to hear from readers about any such items known to them which have not been included. Any errors and omissions must be laid at my own door.

List of Illustrations

Introduction

Note – Places mentioned in the Gazetteer are shown in capitals, e.g. DOVER. For abbreviations see p 147.

South-East England is at present a predominantly agricultural region and much of it is a dormitory area for London. Its industrial archaeology, though widely scattered, is often of considerable age, comprising some industries that would now be regarded as 'heavy' beside many small industries, both urban and rural.

Extractive industries

The oldest industry is the Wealden iron industry which was started before the Roman occupation and was concentrated mainly in the High Weald where the proximity of the iron-bearing Wadhurst Clay, a plentiful supply of charcoal from the extensive forests and the abundance of water for cooling, and later for power supply, produced a natural centre for the process. The early furnaces were bloomeries, producing a spongy form of wrought iron, with slag inclusions, which could be used directly by the smith in his forge. The blast furnace, giving a temperature high enough to liquefy the iron and thus produce cast iron, was introduced in Tudor times and the Weald became one of the two principal suppliers of iron in the country, the other being the Forest of Dean. The main output of the furnaces went into the provision of cannon and shot, prosperity varying with the incidence of wars or periods of peace. After the death of Elizabeth I the industry declined, mainly as result of the rising cost of the fuel – charcoal –

and its death knell was sounded by Abraham Derby's successful smelting of iron with coke as a fuel in 1735 at Coalbrookdale in Shropshire. Thereafter the industry declined more rapidly and the last furnace was blown out at ASHBURNHAM in E Sussex in 1820.

The principal remains of the Wealden iron industry are the hammer ponds which fed the waterwheels for powering the furnace bellows and the trip hammers of the forges. These may be seen at a number of sites, some still in water, others breached or silted up. Good examples of water-filled ponds may be seen in W Sussex at CRABTREE, HANDCROSS and ST LEONARD'S FOREST, and at DANE HILL and MARESFIELD in E Sussex. Ponds where the dam has been breached may be seen at Newbridge Furnace COLEMAN'S HATCH and BECKLEY, both in E Sussex. Very few visible remains of these early furnaces and forges still survive, the masonry wheel-pit at ASHBURNHAM being one of the few relics. A certain number have been excavated, more or less fully, mostly as a rescue operation before being submerged in a reservoir or covered by a car park. One, however, has been taken into guardianship by the Department of the Environment at Pippingford Park, WYCH CROSS in E Sussex, where a well-preserved gun-casting pit was found. Scarlet's Furnace, COWDEN, also in E Sussex, where another gun-casting pit was found, may also be preserved by the owner. The probable location of many early sites can be deduced from the frequent occurrence of the word 'Furnace' or 'Forge' applied to fields, woods, lanes and so on and by the red colour of iron oxide that can still be seen in many small streams.

A considerable number of iron artifacts have survived, the finest collection being at Anne of Cleves House Museum, LEWES, where portions of a waterwheel and a cannon-boring bar are also exhibited. Good collections of iron fire-backs may also be seen at HASTINGS Museum (E Sussex), PETWORTH House (W Sussex) and HASLEMERE Museum (Surrey). Cast-iron grave slabs may be seen at BURWASH, ROTHERFIELD, SALEHURST, SEDLESCOMBE and WADHURST in E Sussex and at WEST HOATHLY in W Sussex.

The West Weald was the site of the principal glass production in England from the mid fourteenth century to the early seventeenth century, rising to a peak about 1600. Its location here may have resulted from the proximity of the Upper and Lower Greensands to a plentiful supply of charcoal in the forests in the West Weald. The industry was concentrated mainly in the parishes of Kirdford and Wisborough Green in W Sussex and Chiddingfold in Surrey. There were also single glass works at Northiam in E Sussex and Knole, near Sevenoaks, in Kent. No visible remains of the glass furnaces are left though their probable location can often be deduced from the names 'Glasshouse' or 'Glass', or their corruptions, applied to fields and copses.

Of the other extractive industries clay pits, serving brick and tile works, and chalk pits, serving lime works for supply to the building industry and agriculture, were widespread. The earliest brick works belonged to the large estates and supplied their whole requirements of building materials. The old brick kilns at ASHBURNHAM still survive, where handmade bricks were fired with wood. Brick-making is known to have occurred on this site at least as early as 1362 but the present

kilns only date from 1840; the last firing took place in 1968 and was fully recorded, together with the history of the brick works. (*SIH* No 1 Winter 1970/71 p 2). A derelict brick works still survives at BERWICK in E Sussex with the walls of three kilns having side-firing holes. The Keymer Brick & Tile Works at BURGESS HILL in W Sussex continues in the old tradition and has several beehive kilns. At SHORTGATE in E Sussex the Halland Brick Works continues to make handmade bricks. The Lunsford Brick Works near Bexhill in E Sussex, which had half-a-dozen beehive kilns operating until recently, was completely demolished in 1977 to make way for a large modern plant.

At one time small lime kilns could be found in many parts of the area, mostly producing lime for agricultural use. Larger kilns may still be seen at DUNCTON and WASHINGTON in W Sussex, at GLYNDE and OFFHAM in E Sussex and at BETCHWORTH, a very large installation, and GOMSHALL, an unusual twentieth-century plant, both in Surrey. Sand was dug in many places for building purposes and for glass-making; there is a notable sand mine at PULBOROUGH in W Sussex and another famous one at DETLING in Kent. Fullers earth, for treating woollen fabrics, was obtained from surface workings near MAIDSTONE and also mined at Nutfield, $c.1\frac{1}{2}$ miles (2·4km) east of Reigate in Surrey. Building stone, mostly sandstone, was also widely quarried in parts of the area; Horsham stone is well known as a roofing material in W Sussex. Extensive mining of the Upper Greensand also occurred at the foot of the North Downs escarpment in E Surrey, from the R. Mole at Dorking eastwards to Godstone; mining continued from the mid-thirteenth century to the end of the nineteenth century, though a few mines were not finally closed until the middle of the twentieth century (*Surrey History* Vol 1 No 3 p 83). Gypsum is also mined at MOUNTFIELD in E Sussex where the Purbeck Beds outcrop. The latest of the extractive industries is in the East Kent coalfield. These are the same coal measures that are worked on the Franco-Belgian border and which, after dipping under the Channel, reappear in the south-east corner of Kent. The seams were discovered in 1882 during test borings by the SER for a proposed Channel tunnel, just west of Shakespeare Cliff near DOVER, though the sinking of shafts there did not start until 1896. The coal measures lie at a considerable depth, between 2,000 and 3,000ft (610 to 914m) and wherever shafts have been sunk severe trouble has been encountered from the ingress of water, often mixed with sand and under a considerable pressure, from the various beds of sand, interspersed with bands of clay, which form deep aquifers below the chalk. Very many shafts were sunk for prospecting by private companies during the late nineteenth and early twentieth centuries, but most came to naught owing to the severe water troubles and great depth, many ceasing for lack of funds before any coal was found. Remains of old unsuccessful mining operations may be seen near DOVER, LYDDEN and COLDRED. Only three collieries are now being worked by the National Coal Board, at Betteshanger, Snowdown and TILMANSTONE, the original shaft and engine house being still in existence at the latter. The architecture of the early twentieth-century mine buildings which still remain is surprisingly similar, all having cast-iron window frames with arched tops, although they were built and owned by different companies. The coal is of good coking quality and is mostly sent to other parts of the country where its special qualities are in demand, even though the Richborough Power Station was specially sited with a view to burning coal from the East Kent field.

Power supplies and services

The main sources of power for early industries were wind-power, water-power and animal-power (including human effort). The major use of wind-power was for corn-milling, and many windmills still survive in varying degrees of dereliction though a far greater number have disappeared. A number have, however, been preserved or restored to full working order and notable examples of post mills may be seen at CHILLENDEN (Kent), OUTWOOD and REIGATE (Surrey), NUTLEY and ROTHERFIELD (E Sussex) and CLAYTON (W Sussex). Good smock mills are to be seen at CRANBROOK, MARGATE and STELLING MINNIS (Kent), PUNNETS TOWN (E Sussex) and SHIPLEY (W Sussex). Tower mills survive at CANTERBURY (Kent), REIGATE (Surrey) and POLEGATE and STONECROSS (E Sussex). Wind-power was also used for drainage and a well-preserved wind pump can be seen in the Open Air Museum at SINGLETON in W Sussex. The remains of a few drainage mills can also be seen at IWADE, OARE and STODMARSH in Kent.

Watermills were once widespread on the many streams and rivers of the area; Domesday Book gives more than 100 in Surrey, more than 150 in Sussex and nearly 350 in Kent. No actual mills survive from this period though the sites of some are known and have been used for milling for many centuries, with the buildings and machinery being replaced from time to time as was necessary. The remains of many eighteenth- and nineteenth-century watermills survive though only a few are still in good order, having been kept working or restored. Good examples may be seen at BUCKLAND, CHEESEMANS GREEN, CHILHAM, EDENBRIDGE, HYTHE and MERSHAM in Kent; at EDENBRIDGE, HURST GREEN, REIGATE and SHALFORD in SURREY; at BURWASH, HELLINGLEY, PLUMPTON and UPPER DICKER in E Sussex and at LINDFIELD, OREHAM COMMON, SAYERS COMMON and TROTTON in W Sussex. Lurgashall Mill is being re-erected at the Open Air Museum at SINGLETON where it should be working again by 1978. An interesting application of water-power is a water-driven saw mill, at BRIGHTLING in E Sussex, which is probably unique to the area and which it is hoped to preserve. In a number of cases the hammer ponds for iron furnaces and forges have been used to drive watermills after the furnace was shut down; mills have also changed their function from time to time, being used for corn-milling, fulling, sawing or paper-making as occasion demanded. Tide mills, operated by impounding water at high tide and releasing it through a waterwheel as the tide ebbed, were established at various tidal inlets round the coast, notably on the tidal creeks of Chichester and Pagham Harbours in W Sussex. The only, fragmentary, remains of a tide mill still to be seen are at Bishopstone near NEWHAVEN in E Sussex.

A plentiful supply of water is necessary for paper-making and mills driven by water-power and producing handmade paper were established during the seventeenth and eighteenth centuries in a number of places in the area, with notable concentrations in the Darent valley in north-east Kent and around MAIDSTONE on the R. Medway and in the valleys of the Len and Loose to the east and south of the town. Only one still survives, making high-quality handmade paper, Hayle Mill in the Loose valley, where there has been a long tradition of paper-making. The manufacture of gunpowder was another industry that required water for processing and gunpowder works were established during the sixteenth and seventeenth centuries at several places in the area: between Battle and Crowhurst in E Sussex, at Chilworth near ALBURY in Surrey and the very important ones at FAVERSHAM in Kent, where one of the old grinding mills is being restored.

Animal-power, using horses or donkeys, has been used from early times for supplying power on farms and for raising water from wells. A good example of a small portable horse-gin for use on a farm may be seen at the Agricultural Museum at WILMINGTON Priory in E Sussex and a larger, fixed one has been re-erected at the Open Air Museum at SINGLETON. There is also a good example at the Agricultural Museum at BROOK in Kent. Donkey wheels for raising water from wells may be seen at GODMERSHAM in Kent, at FRISTON and STANMER in E Sussex and at POYNINGS in W Sussex. Good examples of horse-gins for water pumping from wells may be seen at CHILHAM Castle, OTTERDEN and RAINHAM in Kent, at PRESTON and STANMER in E Sussex and at LINDFIELD and PATCHING in W Sussex. Human labour was occasionally used as a source of power in times of water shortage and there is an eighteenth-century treadmill crane on the wharf at GUILDFORD in Surrey.

When water was to be pumped up from a river, a waterwheel could be used to operate the pumps. One of the best examples of this is at Coultershaw Bridge, just south of PETWORTH, where a water-driven pump, dating from the second half of the eighteenth century, is being restored to full working order. A similar nineteenth-century water-driven pump, but on a smaller scale, is still working on private land at Abinger near GOMSHALL, and nineteenth-century pumps, in this case driven by a water turbine, can be seen at ARUNDEL in W Sussex. At a later date steam engines were installed for water pumping on a larger scale and the finest example of this is to be seen at the Engineerium at HOVE in E Sussex, where a late nineteenth-century beam engine is now under steam again, though not pumping water. Two small nineteenth-century beam engines and their water pumps are preserved at ASHFORD in Kent though no longer used. An early twentieth-century, triple-expansion steam engine is still kept for standby use in the water-pumping station at BREDE in E Sussex. Small installations, usually driven by a gas or oil engine but occasionally by a waterwheel, which once supplied water to large private houses or farms, may still be found; one such is at BRASTED CHART in Kent and another at EWHURST in E Sussex.

Of the other possible sources of power the very few remains of the natural gas industry at HEATHFIELD in E Sussex are of interest. Since the advent of natural gas from the North Sea over most of the area the older coal-gas works have almost completely vanished; the late nineteenth-century gas holders at Hastings still remain, unused, though due for demolition. An early twentieth-century electricity-generating station still stands at PORT-SLADE in W Sussex, though now shut down, probably gutted and due for demolition. The SE Electricity Board have, however, created a most interesting museum of early distribution equipment and domestic appliances at TON-BRIDGE in Kent.

Transport

The most useful early form of trans-port was by water and in the late eighteenth and early nineteenth centuries the increasing need to supply food to London and coal, lime and other commodities to the country districts in the area led to intensive efforts to improve and extend the navigation of the rivers. The Arun, Adur, Eastern and Western Rothers, Ouse, Stour, Medway, Darent, Mole and Wey all received attention. The Arun and the Wey had already been made navigable for some distance from their mouths in the seventeenth and eighteenth centuries and a canal to link them, the Wey & Arun Canal, was completed in 1816 and extended to Portsmouth by the Portsmouth & Arundel Canal in 1823 which only lasted until the 1840s. Interesting remains of this navigation can be seen at HARDHAM, NORTH HEATH and WISBOROUGH GREEN in W Sussex, at BRAMLEY, PYRFORD and SEND in Surrey and at various other places. What is left of the Portsmouth & Arundel Canal can be seen at BIRDHAM and HUNSTON in W Sussex. The Wey & Arun Canal, after official closure in 1871, is being currently restored by the Wey & Arun Canal Trust who have already achieved much in the way of improvements and rebuilding.

The Basingstoke Canal, which linked London to Basingstoke but proceeded no further, was built between 1788 and 1794, thus pre-dating the Wey & Arun by more than 20 years. After many vicissitudes, through commercial traffic finally ceased in the early years of the twentieth century; it does not appear ever to have been formally closed and it is now being restored by a voluntary body. The more interesting features of its remains may be seen at BROOKWOOD, MYTCHETT, WOKING and WOODHAM in Surrey. The Thames & Medway Canal, between Gravesend and Rochester, built in 1824 to cut off the long and tortuous journey round the Isle of Grain, though short has an unusually large tunnel which, when the canal was closed in 1846, enabled the SER to run a double-track line through it. The southern exit of the tunnel can be seen across the terminal basin at Frindsbury near ROCHESTER. Parts of the canal are still in water and there is a swing bridge over the sea lock at GRAVESEND. At DARTFORD in Kent there are two small swing bridges over the R. Darent with hand operation and the method of operating the gates of the sea lock is unusual.

The Royal Military Canal, built between 1804 and 1809, was a purely defensive measure, being designed both to oppose an enemy advancing across Romney Marsh and to provide easy transport for troops and materials to wherever they were needed. Its defensive character is plainly shown by the kink about every 600yd (548m) to allow enfilading fire down each stretch. It runs from Hythe in Kent to Cliff End, between Rye and Hastings in E Sussex, and comprises a canal, military road, towpath and drains on both sides. An artificial cut from Hythe to IDEN where it joins the Eastern Rother, it makes use of this river and the R. Brede as far as Winchelsea and then continues as an artificial cut to its western terminus at Cliff End, where the remains of the old sea lock can still be seen on the beach at low tide. Tidal locks exist at PLAYDEN on the Rother and at RYE on the Brede.

The coastal ports have always been important for cross-channel and coastal shipping, as well as naval purposes, and considerable works were carried out in the eighteenth and nineteenth centuries to improve facilities. The movement of shingle along the South Coast and silting of the estuaries and harbours has always been a problem and has caused the decline of several ports. The main estuarine ports are ARUNDEL, LITTLEHAMPTON and SHOREHAM in W Sussex, LEWES, NEWHAVEN and RYE in E Sussex, and Sandwich, FAVERSHAM, ROCHESTER, CHATHAM, GRAVESEND and DARTFORD in Kent. Folkestone, DOVER, RAMSGATE and WHITSTABLE in Kent are the result of extensive harbour works, though DOVER was a small estuarine port in Roman times. Old warehouses, boatstores, piers, jetties and other harbour facilities may be seen at most of these and a Fairbairn hand-operated crane is preserved at Dover. Important naval establishments have existed at Dover, CHATHAM and SHEERNESS.

Until the end of the seventeenth century road communications were poor in the area, being particularly bad in the heavy clay of the Weald. Considerable improvements came about as a result of the various Turnpike Acts in the eighteenth century, which set up trusts to construct proper roads with powers to levy tolls for the use of them, there being about 50 separate trusts in each of Kent and Sussex. The General Turnpike Act of 1766 obliged all trusts to erect mile posts on their turnpikes and many of these still survive, together with a number of toll houses though both are much subject to demolition as a result of modern road-widening activities. A number of old toll houses still remain, however, sometimes incorporated into larger buildings. They were usually small, single-storey buildings and may often be recognized by their position on the edge of the road and the small observation windows, now usually bricked up, which enabled the toll-keeper to watch out for traffic approaching along the road. Interesting examples may be seen at BATTLE, LEWES, RINGMER and WADHURST in E Sussex, CLAPHAM, NORTHCHAPEL, SHOREHAM and STORRINGTON in W Sussex, ESHER and

WALTON in Surrey, and BIDDENDEN, BISHOPSBOURNE, CHARING and SHELD-WICH in Kent. The old toll bridges at SHOREHAM in W Sussex and WALTON in Surrey still remain though now only used for foot traffic. The swing bridge at LITTLEHAMPTON in W Sussex still survives, though threatened with demolition, but the similar one at Newhaven has now been demolished to reduce the obstruction to river traffic; a full record of it was however made before demolition. A considerable number of mile posts survive and there are several nearly unbroken runs of these, notably in E Sussex extending into Kent and Surrey (see beginning of E Sussex gazetteer), on A3 from ESHER through COBHAM and RIPLEY to SEND in Surrey, and on A28 and A290 in Kent (see beginning of Kent gazetteer). Unusual isolated mile posts may be seen at ASHBURNHAM, LEWES, SHEFFIELD PARK and WYCH CROSS in E Sussex and at ESHER and GODSTONE in Surrey. The old road bridges at LEWES in E Sussex, STOPHAM in W Sussex, COBHAM in Surrey and AYLESFORD in Kent are worth looking at.

The coming of railways to the region was marked by competition between the LB & SCR, who had virtually a monopoly of west and central Sussex, and the L & SWR in the north west of the area, and particularly by a very bitter feud between the SER and the LC & DR in north and east Kent, which was only resolved by their amalgamation as the SE & CR at the end of the nineteenth century. In the west of the area many branch and secondary lines were built which were never a success commercially and have now been closed, while the feud in Kent resulted in a number of competing lines, which it was obvious from the start could never be a success, and which were abandoned later. It is still possible to walk along stretches of the abandoned lines, notably the Shoreham–Christ's Hospital–Guildford line most of which has been designated a public bridleway; the bridge across the R. Arun at BUCKS GREEN in W Sussex and the station at BAYNARDS in Surrey are worth visiting. Much of the Elham Valley line in Kent can also be followed and the tunnels at BRIDGE and ETCHINGHILL are worth a visit; such stations as remain on this line are now used as private dwellings. The Chichester–Midhurst line has interesting station remains at LAVANT, SINGLETON and COCKING, the two latter being privately owned and having some attractive incised plaster decoration on the walls. PETWORTH Station on the Midhurst–Pulborough line is a fine example of LB & SCR wooden buildings for country stations; it is threatened by development and it is hoped to preserve it, either on site or by transfer to a suitable Open Air Industrial Museum to be established in the old chalk pits behind AMBERLEY station. Pleasant old station buildings still in use may be seen at BATTLE and RYE in E Sussex and at CANTERBURY West in Kent. On the Canterbury–Whitstable line, the second oldest railway in Britain, having been opened in 1830, the Tyler Hill Tunnel just N. of CANTERBURY may be inspected and the abutments of the reputed oldest railway bridge in the country may be seen on the S edge of WHITSTABLE. Two stretches of main line have been preserved and are operated by preservation societies, the Bluebell Line from SHEFFIELD PARK to HORSTED KEYNES and the Kent & East Sussex Railway from TENTERDEN to BODIAM, this line being the first to be built under the Light Railway Order. A short stretch of the narrow-gauge railway originally laid down by Bowaters has been preserved and opened to the public at

SITTINGBOURNE in Kent. Volks Electric Railway along BRIGHTON front was the first public electric railway in the country, being opened in 1883, and is still in operation. The Romney, Hythe & Dymchurch Railway in Kent, with headquarters at NEW ROMNEY and running from Hythe to Dungeness, is more than a toy, having been opened in 1927, more than 50 years ago, with the full support of the SR.

At one time a number of cliff railways existed along the coast, mostly operating on the water-balance principle, where the weight of a full water tank beneath the descending car was used to draw up the ascending car whose water tank was empty. Control was by brakes either on the car or at the upper end where the rope joining the cars passed over a large pulley. Such railways were installed at HASTINGS in E Sussex, and at FOLKESTONE, BROADSTAIRS and MARGATE in Kent. Two of the three original ones at Folkestone, serving the Metropole Hotel and Sandgate Hill, have been closed and the tracks lifted or left derelict; the remaining one is unique in being a double one with four cars and four tracks. Of the installations that remain all are now electrified, the water-balance principle having been abandoned in the interests of public safety. The only water-balance cliff railway still in operation in the country is at Lynton on the N Devon coast. Another unusual railway was the Devil's Dyke branch line at HOVE, which, though a standard gauge railway, had an average gradient of 1:40; its course can still be traced for most of its length. Nothing is now left of the Devil's Dyke Steep Grade Railway which ran from Poynings to the top of the Devil's Dyke at gradients varying between 1:1·5 and 1:2·9. It was a true cliff railway with two cars on an endless rope operated by an oil engine at the upper terminus. A few remains of the Surrey Iron Railway, a pre-locomotive line built in 1803, can be seen at MERSTHAM though the rails preserved there are not on the line of the original track which was lifted in 1838.

Miscellaneous industries

Before the days of refrigeration icehouses were extensively used by large country houses and estates. They comprise a deep brick-lined well surmounted by a domed, or sometimes pyramidal, roof with an entrance passage, sometimes a long curved one, fitted with two doors to form an airlock and prevent the ingress of heat. Ice was cut in the winter from neighbouring shallow ponds, often constructed for the purpose, and stacked in the well on a bed of straw and covered with straw. There was usually a hole in the roof for the withdrawal of ice for domestic use during the summer and the chamber could also be used for the storage of game and other perishable food. A drain was provided at the bottom of the well to take away melt water and the whole building was commonly built into a bank or partly covered with earth to insulate it thermally. Good examples can be seen at BOGNOR and PETWORTH in W Sussex, at EAST CLANDON and MICKLEHAM in Surrey and at LAMBERHURST in Kent. There are also fine examples at Bromley, just over the border in Greater London.

Agriculture has always been one of the main industries in the area and items illustrating its history can be seen in many places. Barns of all types and ages occur widely in the country, though often in poor condition; a particularly fine specimen is the old barn at ALCISTON in E Sussex, once the tithe barn of Battle Abbey. A very fine collection of agricultural implements and machines is to be seen at the museum at WILMINGTON Priory in E Sussex and a further good collection is at the Wye Agricultural College's museum at BROOK in Kent. Oast houses, for drying hops, are to be seen all over E Sussex and Kent, most of them now converted to private dwellings or used for storage and consequently gutted inside. A particularly fine set is to be seen at LAMBERHURST in Kent, where they have been well preserved though converted for dwellings. Oast houses in their original condition with firing holes and drying floors intact still survive at BROOK in Kent and at EWHURST and NEWICK in E Sussex. Old farm waggons can be seen at Norton's Farm near BEAUPORT PARK and at Michelham Priory near UPPER DICKER, both in E Sussex. A small nineteenth-century farm, complete with all its buildings, survives at HIGH HURSTWOOD and is preserved by the owner with the intention of farming it again.

Blacksmiths' shops still survive in several places supplying horseshoes for riding stables, repairing farm machinery and making ornamental ironwork. A particularly interesting one is still working intermittently at BOARS-HEAD near Crowborough in E Sussex; the smith is 90 years old and is probably the last maker of handmade edge tools in the south. A reconstructed forge may be seen at SINGLETON, in the Open Air Museum, where a wheelwright's shop is also being reconstructed. Wheelwrights' shops are also still working at Ashford and Paddock Wood in Kent. Charcoal burning was once widespread in the forests of the Weald and a charcoal burners' camp has been reconstructed at SINGLETON. The trade is still carried on, using modern methods, near Battle. Salt-panning was done at several points along the south coast but practically nothing now remains of this industry.

The sole surviving conical pottery kiln in the area still stands at PIDDINGHOE near Newhaven in E Sussex.

Small engineering workshops survive in several towns, notably at BRIGHTON, and a builder's workshop, now kept as a museum, can be seen at NORTHIAM in E Sussex which houses one of the finest collections of moulding planes in the country. At GODALMING in Surrey there is a most interesting engineering workshop with a very large lathe and also the large water turbine, gearing and part of the shafting which once supplied power to the factory. An old foundry crane at THAMES DITTON had been dismantled to avoid demolition and is now in store awaiting a suitable final home.

Early airfields exist at Shoreham and FORD in W Sussex, the former still in use but the latter disused and partly converted to a factory estate. The old aircraft factory and Brooklands motor-racing track at Byfleet in Surrey are well known. In the field of communications the old Admiralty Telegraph from London to Portsmouth, for passing signals by semaphore from one point to another, has left its mark in the Telegraph Tower at OCKHAM in Surrey. A few buildings still survive in the area and the sites of others may sometimes be deduced from such names as Telegraph Hill and Telegraph Lane still to be found in various places. Further examples of the Admiralty Telegraph buildings still survive in Hampshire. Examples of small-scale generation of electricity by water-power may be seen at Park Mill BURWASH in E Sussex, at Gibbons Mill BUCKS GREEN in W Sussex and at several other places.

Gazetteer

The sites in this gazetteer are listed in alphabetical order, in terms of the nearest place shown on the relevant ¼in OS map. Owing to the ravages of dereliction and the activities of the bulldozer it is possible that some of the sites listed may have disappeared by the time this gazetteer is in print; one or two have vanished while it was in preparation.

Kent

The longest and most important river in Kent is the Medway, whose estuary extends from the Thames to beyond Rochester. The first lock occurs between Aylesford and Maidstone and the river is navigable for small boats as far as Tonbridge. There is much of interest for the industrial archaeologist in the early naval bases at Sheerness and Chatham and the ports of Rochester and Maidstone, although demolition and rebuilding has removed much of interest in the latter town. The basin of the Medway extends into Surrey and E Sussex and many watermills are situated on the river and its tributaries.

Several good series of mile posts survive on the turnpike roads. On A28, at Thannington (TR123563), Chartham (TR110554 and TR094554), Chilham (TR083542 and TR074531), Godmersham (TR073514 and TR062503, the latter without its plate), Bilting (TR053491), Boughton Aluph (TR040480) and Boughton Less (TR033467), at Great Chart (TQ991425, TQ976417 and TQ968403) and Bethesden (TQ958394, TQ941396 and TQ926399); on A290 at Blean (TR126601), Honey Hill (TR117614 and TR110628) and at Whitstable (TR105643). On A2 mile posts may still be seen at Temple Ewell (TR291440), Lydden (TR274451, TR260454, TR249466, TR236476 and TR226488), and at Bridge (TR186538 and TR176551). A number of mile posts on this road have already disappeared as a result of road widening and straightening and more will probably go in the future.

The Elham valley line from Canterbury to Folkestone was built by the SER between 1887 and 1889 in answer to a threatened connection between the two towns by the LC & DR. It served a number of villages in the Elham valley and, although losing most of its traffic to bus routes after World War I was kept in operation during World War II to provide accommodation for 'Boche Buster', an 18in gun, and two other 12in guns, on special railway waggons, which were intended to fire on the German lines in occupied France. 'Boche Buster' was only fired three times, recoiling 20ft (6·1m) when fired, and the other two were never fired. All three were removed in 1944 and the line was finally closed in 1947 and the track lifted. Part of the line can still be walked and the tunnels at Bishopsbourne and Etchinghill visited.

APPLEDORE

Railway station, TQ975298. This station, near the junction of the line to Dungeness, lies isolated in Romney Marsh 1¼ miles (2km) from the village. A good example of an SER station which has survived with practically no alteration since its building in 1881. The line to near Dungeness is still in occasional use.

ASHFORD

Railway engines, TR022415. At the South Eastern Steam Centre in Hunter Avenue an interesting collection of old locomotives and rolling stock is housed. Restoration work on these is steadily proceeding and some of them are under steam occasionally on a short length of track adjacent to the centre.

Water mill, TQ989449. The mill

1   Ashford: beam engine for water pumping

stands on the NE side of A20 *c*.2 miles (3·2km) on the London side of Ashford. A 4-storey brick and timber building, now used as a store, it has the remains of an iron overshot wheel and mostly iron gearing with 2 pairs of stones; also a lucam and sack hoist. Mid-19th century.

Water-pumping station, TR019488. From the Ring Road go straight on down A292 (Hythe Road), over the river, 2nd turning left (Deering Road), right at end of road (Wallis Road). The Mid-Kent Water Co's Depot is on the left in 50yd (46m). A 19th-century brick building with round-headed, cast-iron window frames houses two small compound rotative beam engines (*Plate 1*) driving 3-throw triple-barrel pumps *c*.10ft (3m) below floor level delivering water from wells or bores. The engines are self-standing, the beams *c*.9ft (2·75 m) long, being supported on single fluted cast-iron pillars *c*.7ft (2·1m) high. The HP cylinder is

c.13in (33cm) diameter with a stroke of *c*.18in (46cm), the LP cylinder *c*.22in (56cm) diameter with a stroke of *c*.26in (66cm). The flywheel is *c*.10ft (3m) diameter and the pump of 17in (43cm) stroke is driven through a 1:3·25 reduction gear, the large wheel *c*.6ft (1·8m) diameter being cast iron with wooden teeth on one pump and all cast iron on the other one. Both engines were made by Thomas Horn & Sons, Westminster. The beams are 10in (25·4cm) deep at the centre and 6½in (16·5cm) wide. Both engines have governors driven from the main shaft by bevel gears and belt drive. The boiler is missing though the chimney of the boiler house remains. Both engines are preserved by the owners, the Mid-Kent Water Co.

AYLESFORD

Road bridge, TQ729589. A side road leading to the village crosses the R.

2 Aylesford: road bridge

Medway at a point where the lowest ford on the river existed. The bridge, a narrow one-way structure with pedestrian refuges over the main piers, dates from the 14th century but the centre arch was enlarged early in the 19th century to give better access for river traffic. The best view of it is obtained from the modern bridge just to the E of it (*Plate 2*).

BENENDEN

Windmill, TQ821325. On N side of B2086 *c.*1 mile (1·6km) E of the village. A ruinous smock mill, without sweeps or stone. Built *c.*1900, it ran until the early years of this century.

BIDBOROUGH

Windmill, TQ562435. On S side of B2176. The stump of an 18th-century tower mill, with machinery only on the lower floor. It ceased work *c.*1900.

BIDDENDEN

Toll house, TQ855395. On A274 at Curteis Corner, *c.*350yd (320m) S of its junction with B2077 (*Plate 3*).

BISHOPSBOURNE

Disused railway station, TR185525. On the Elham Valley Railway, built in 1887, which ran from Canterbury to Cheriton, just W of Folkestone. The station building is now a private dwelling.

BRASTED

Village pump, TQ474552. In middle of village green; an octagonal cast-iron pump of Gothic design with a spout in

3 Biddenden: the observation window indicates a probable toll house

the shape of an animal's head.

BRASTED CHART

Water pump, TQ460535. On private land approached through the grounds of Valence School, S of A25 about half-way between Brasted and Westerham. A 16ft (4·88m) diameter iron water-wheel, fed from a large pond, drove through gearing 2 single-cylinder force pumps that originally supplied water to a number of the surrounding farms. The waterwheel and gearing are sub-stantially intact (*Plate 4*) and are being cleaned and renovated by boys from a school in Sevenoaks. The pump cylin-ders, air chamber and pipe work are also intact but unfortunately the con-necting rods and pump cylinder covers have been removed and the pump rod guides broken, though portions of the two connecting rods were found buried in rubbish at the bottom of the pump pit, from which it has been possible to reconstruct the original arrangement.

BRIDGE

Bourne Park tunnel, TQ178530–180528. The S end of this tunnel on the now abandoned Elham Valley Railway may be reached easily from Lenhall Farm and the N end by walk-ing for about 600yd (548m) along the cutting from a bridge over the track. The tunnel is 330yd (302m) long, brick built, and constructed by the cut-and-cover method by Thomas Walker in 1888. It is double track, on a slight curve with an elliptical arch *c.*15ft (4·6m) wide × 25ft (7·6m) high and has several safety recesses in the sides. It is in good condition. Consider-able stretches of the Elham Valley Railway, from Canterbury to Folke-

4   Brasted Chart: waterwheel drive to pumps

stone, are accessible to walkers, though the track is much overgrown and very muddy in places.

Old railway station, TR173544. On the Elham Valley Railway $c.\frac{1}{2}$ mile (800m) W of A2, on a minor road N of the village. The platform still remains and the station building is now a private dwelling. The station approach is just before the abutment of a good, brick-built skew bridge which carried the railway over the road.

Toll cottage, TR192531. On W side of A2 1 mile (1·6km) SE of village at turning to Bishopsbourne. An octagonal cottage with thatched roof and octagonal castellated central chimney, probably 18th century (*Plate 5*). It has a bay window with pointed top and leaded glass on side towards road.

BROADSTAIRS

Cliff railway, TR397678. A single-car railway running for $c.$100ft (30·5m) through the chalk cliff face from Albion Street down to Viking Bay. It is electrically operated and is of 5ft 3in (1·6m) gauge.

BROOK

Agricultural Museum, TR006443. This museum belongs to Wye Agricultural College and is open on Wednesday afternoons from June to September and on Saturday afternoons in August. It houses a fine collection of farm implements, carts and waggons though in a rather confined space; also a good horse-gin (*Plate 6*) and an oast house which has been fully restored so that the construction and operation of this may be easily seen.

BUCKLAND

Watermill, TR297432. Crabble Mill lies on the R. Dour just SW of A2, $c.$2

5   Bridge: toll house

miles (3·2km) from the front at Dover. It is an exceptionally fine breast-shot mill built during the Napoleonic Wars at the turn of the 18th/19th centuries. There are 2 weatherboarded storeys, with lucam, above 3 brick storeys, with breastshot wheel, 5 pairs of stones with governors and extensive auxilliary machinery including a large bolter. The mill ceased work in 1890 but has been fully restored by the Cleary Foundation; it is now leased by the Dover Town Council and open to the public on Wednesday afternoons and at weekends from May to September.

Watermill, TR309425. The old Buckland flour mill on the R. Dour is on the north-east side of A2 *c.*1 mile (1·6km) from the front at Dover. Built *c.*1815 it comprises a 4-storey weatherboarded section with lucam and an adjacent later 5-storey brick-built section. The wheel has gone but the waterways remain. The 5-storey section built in 1876 was a steam-driven mill. Milling

ceased in 1957.

CANTERBURY

Depository, TR148573. Pickford's Depository. Opposite Canterbury East Station. Late 19th century. The building appears to be little used now and may be due for demolition as the adjacent house was demolished in 1975.

Lime works and quarry, TR148567. The Dane-John Lime Works just S of the city was bisected by the Elham Valley line when this was built in 1889. An extensive system of 2ft (61cm)-gauge mineral lines was laid down to transport chalk from the quarry faces to the kilns; operation was mainly by winch on inclined tracks. The quarry is now derelict though the sites of the kilns and some of the tracks can still be seen.

Maltings, TR152574. On the corner of Oaten Hill Place and Oaten Hill. A

6   Brook: horse-gin – note drive shaft to wall of barn

19th-century 2-storey brick building with tiled roof and 2 cowled oasts on top. There is a hoist on the first floor on the front.

Old engine, TR149575. In Dane John Gardens the 'Invicta' is preserved on a section of standard gauge rail on a concrete plinth. Built by George Stephenson she was listed No 12, the 'Rocket' being No 11. On 3 May 1830 she drew the first train on the Canterbury–Whitstable Railway and worked on this line for many years.

Pumping station, TR138567. Thannington Water Pumping Station of the Mid-Kent Water Co. On S side of A28 (Caterbury–Maidstone). The building dates from 1869 but was extended in 1924. Both dates are on plaques on the building. The pumps are now electrically driven with diesel engines as standby.

Railway tunnel, TR140602–TR143595. Tyler Hill tunnel on the disused Caterbury–Whitstable line is the oldest railway tunnel in the country, having been opened in the spring of 1830. The tunnel goes under Christchurch College, the S entrance being in the college grounds. The N entrance can be reached from a footpath. The line was closed at the end of 1952, and the tunnel is now boarded up at both ends and is believed to have collapsed in the middle.

Warehouse, TR147581. On NW side of Pound Lane. A stone and flint 2-storey building with large central door on ground floor and timber structure above this with door and hoist.

Warehouse, TR149580. On SW side of Orange Street. A 19th-century 2-storey brick building with pantiled roof and a hoist on the first floor.

Warehouse, TR151572. On NW side of Nunnery Fields at junction with Lansdown Road. An 18th-century brick building with weatherboarded

7   Canterbury: West Station

extension at rear. Tiled roof with projecting dormer window containing a hoist. Ground floor now a Post Office and Store.

Warehouse, TR146582. At No 6 North Lane. A 2-storey brick building with hipped, tiled roof. An iron crane is mounted beside the first floor doorway and above the door is a tablet reading 'H.W.M. / 1824'.

Watermill, TR156588. Barton Mill is the sole surviving medieval mill in the city. A 4-storey timber building spanning the R. Great Stour it is mostly an early 19th-century rebuild but early 13th-century work survives on the ground floor and in the roof. Modern milling machinery was installed early in the 20th century, at first steam-driven and converted to electric drive in 1937, but the original machinery is still preserved and operable though no longer used.

The Weavers, TR148579. On NE side of St Peter's Street. A restored timber-framed building dating from c.1500 which was a workshop of the Huguenot weavers. The ground floor has modern shop fronts on the street side.

West Railway Station, TR146584. This SER station, built in 1846, is a pleasant single-storey building with an elegant classical portico at the entrance (*Plate 7*). The Canterbury–Whitstable line used a bay at the N end of the down platform. A fine red-brick warehouse faces the station entrance.

Windmill, TR161578. On N side of A257 on W edge of the town. Canterbury's only tower mill, it dates from 1817 and has been preserved and used as a private dwelling. The windshaft and brake wheel exist and the stocks, but no sweeps.

CHARING

Toll house, TQ946484. On B2077 c.½ mile (800m) S of the railway bridge.

Windmill, TQ958502. On N side of A252 to E of the village, on the brow of Charing Hill. Dating from c.1900 it is in good repair, though lacking sweeps. The windshaft and drive to the spur wheel remain. It stopped work c.1891.

CHARING HEATH

Watermill, TQ913491. This mill lies on the R. Great Stour c.1 mile (1·6km) W of the village. The mill is derelict though most of the overshot wheel and some of the wooden machinery remain. It dates from c.1865.

CHARTHAM

Watermill, TR097554. A submerged water turbine still remains with some of the cast-iron gearing on the first floor. There are also some eel traps remaining in the river.

CHART SUTTON

Watermill, TQ794493. Now a private dwelling but the remains of an iron overshot wheel may still be seen though all the internal machinery has gone.

CHATHAM

Boat store, TQ765700. No 53 boat store was built in 1813 for repairing and building naval vessels.

CHEESEMAN'S GREEN

Watermill, TR039388. Swanton Mill, on the R. East Stour c.¾ mile (1·2km) W of Mersham Mill. The mill has been fully restored and now grinds again; it is preserved as a museum of milling and is open to the public at weekends from June to September. At the end of a lane going E from a minor road running S from Sevington.

CHIDDINGSTONE

Iron grave slabs, TQ501452. There are two interesting cast-iron grave slabs in the floor of Chiddingstone Church. One in the nave covers the grave of Richard Streatfeild, owner of the neighbouring Chiddingstone Castle, who died on 15 September 1601, while the other in the south aisle marks the grave of Thomas Basset of London who died on 13 January 1715.
Watermill, TQ496461. A disused mill now used for farm storage. The building still stands but is not in very good repair. The wheel pit, sluice and lucam can still be seen but no machinery is left.

CHILHAM

Horse-gin, TR065534. In Chilham Castle, a fine example under a tiled roof at the edge of the castle keep. It has an overhead gear-wheel and a 3-throw pump.
Watermill, TR077536. On A28, 100yd (91m) SW of junction with A252, a lane on the E side leads over an unattended level crossing to the mill on the R. Great Stour. The mill is owned by the Mid-Kent Water Co, who have preserved the mill, though it is no longer operable. The building is of 5 storeys, brick on the ground floor and weatherboarded above with a lucam, all painted white and in good condition. Attached to the side of the building is a 2-storey wheel-house containing a cast-iron, breast-shot wheel with a cruciform shaft, three 8-armed spiders and sheet-iron buckets. The wooden sluice-gate is in good condition. The mill is a large one, containing on the 1st floor 5 pairs of underdrift stones driven from the great spur wheel and 1 pair overdrift, driven by a belt off a vertical shaft, which is driven from the rim of the crown wheel mounted above the great spur wheel. On the 2nd floor there are a wire machine, bolter and dresser, together with elevator feeding them, which are belt-driven from a layshaft on the same floor. The 3rd floor contains grain bins and the 4th floor more bins, the main sack hoist inside the mill and the hoist in the lucam. All pairs of stones and their casings remain, and the machinery is generally in good condition. The mill dates from the 2nd half of the 19th century and ceased working in 1933. The mill house adjoins the mill.

CHILLENDEN

Windmill, TR269543. On N side of road between Goodnestone and Chillenden. A post mill with open trestle, built 1868. Owned by Kent County Council and kept in good repair. Machinery intact as far as stones, but no auxiliary equipment. Four patent sails with elliptical springs but no shutters. The body has been reinforced underneath with iron struts and angles which now prevent it turning; no fantail, but tail pole and cartwheel. Ceased work in 1949.

COLDRED

Abandoned colliery, TR280470. The remains of Guilford Colliery are on a narrow road running NW from Whitfield. From 1906 onwards 3 shafts were sunk but are now sealed off inside circular brick walls c.6ft (1·8m) high; the foundations of the engine houses for these shafts remain but the whole of this area is heavily overgrown and very difficult of access. The most prominent feature of the site is a very large and handsome brick engine house (*Plate 8*), SE of the remains just mentioned, in fairly good condition with all the supporting walls for the engine and winding gear. The shaft for this would have been on the SW side but was never sunk. The workshops in fairly good condition, and the offices, rather derelict, still remain, also the powder magazine, a small brick building c.300yd (274m) to the W. Two of the shafts were sunk to a depth of c.1250ft (381m) and a borehole was sunk to 1346ft (410m) without reaching the coal measures. Severe trouble from water ingress was always experienced and 'cementation' was tried unsuccessfully between 1919 and 1920 before the site was finally abandoned in 1921 without mining any coal. The East Kent Railway ran a single track branch line to the colliery from Eythorne in 1906 and the course of this can still be traced in a few places, though the track has been lifted.

CRANBROOK

Toll cottage, TQ798365. On an island site at Golford crossroads c.2 miles (3·2km) E of the town. A single-storey brick building with tiled roof and weatherboarded gables. A modern extension on the E side is being carried out to match the existing construction. It dates from 1761 and has a small projecting window on the N side for the collection of tolls.

Windmill, TQ779359. Kent's most famous mill and the tallest mill in the county. This octagonal smock mill on a very high brick base rises to 72ft (22m) to the top of the cap. Standing on a hill in the centre of the town, it is a landmark for miles (*Plate 9*). It was built by Henry Dobell in 1814, as a stone tablet over the door records, and another stone tablet records that John Russell was miller from 1918 to 1956. When built it had common sails and no fantail but these were replaced by patent sails and a fantail added in

8   Coldred: engine house at Guilford Colliery

9   Cranbrook: smock mill, the tallest in Kent

1840. Standby power was provided by a steam engine in 1863, a gas engine in 1919 and an electric motor in 1954. The mill is in full working order, with 2 of the original 3 pairs of stones. The present sweeps are unusual, having the steel stock and pair of whips in one piece, which is a Dutch design, but with English patent sails whereas the Dutch ones would be plain sails. Only animal feed is produced. The mill is open to the public.

CROCKHAM HILL

Mile post, TQ442503. A plain iron mile post $c.\frac{1}{4}$ mile (400m) S of the village on B2026 (see EAST SUSSEX B2026 mile posts).

DARTFORD

Lock and bridges, TQ540750 (lock) and TQ543746 (bridges). To reach these old bascule bridges and tidal lock on the R. Darent go past Dartford Station and after passing under the railway go straight on down a cul-de-sac. Near the end of this a path on the right leads past an old weatherboarded cottage to the 1st bridge (for foot passengers) over the river. Beyond this bridge the 2nd bridge (for vehicles) lies to the right, and a path on the left beside the river leads in about $\frac{1}{4}$ mile (400m) to the tidal lock. The bridges are single-leaf bascule type, and are hand-operated via a bevel gear, a worm drive and a pinion acting on the toothed quadrant on the bridge (*Plate 10*) there being 2 quadrants on the footbridge which is 45ft (13·7m) long by 7ft (2·1m) wide with the shaft 6ft (1·8m) from the end and 1 on the vehicle bridge which is 30ft (9·1m) long by 10ft (3m) wide with the shaft 10ft (3m) from the end. The footbridge is a public footpath and is fully operable, but on the vehicle bridge the bevel gear

and worm drive are missing. As the bridge leads only to the island site of a demolished factory it may possibly be due for demolition or replacement. The tidal lock with weir and spillway adjacent to it has mitre gates at both the upper and lower ends, with an unusual operating gear for these. They are opened and closed by a pinion operating on a toothed quadrant, the drive to the pinion being from a handle and bevel gear mounted on a cast-iron pillar alongside (*Plate 11*).

DEAL

Timeball tower, TR377526. Built in 1812 as an Admiralty signal station during the Napoleonic wars it was converted in 1855 to a Timeball tower to provide a Greenwich time signal to ships in the Downs. A square, 4-storey stuccoed brick tower with a mast on top, on which a 14ft (4·27m) diameter copper ball was raised half-way up at 12·55 pm, to the top at 12.58 pm, and dropped at 01.00 pm by an electric signal from Greenwich where a similar timeball had been installed in 1833 for the benefit of ships in the Thames. The tower stands on the land-ward side of Beach Street.

DETLING

Sand mine, TQ781572. At Newnham Court Farm just W of the junction of A249 with A20 (the Maidstone bypass). Sand was quarried here for several centuries for glass-making and domestic purposes. The mines are very extensive and in the 18th century, after extraction had ceased, guided tours were arranged.

DOVER

Disused coal pits, TR296393. At base of cliffs where the Dover–Folkestone

10 Dartford: mechanism of bascule bridge

line emerges from its tunnel under Shakespeare Cliff. Coal was discovered here in 1882 during test-boring by the SER for a proposed Channel tunnel. From 1896 onwards 3 shafts were sunk to a depth of *c*.1600ft (488m). Severe trouble was experienced from the ingress of water and the only coal dispatched from these pits was a train of 12 10-ton (10·2 tonnes) trucks in 1912. The site was abandoned for coal in 1914, though some ironstone continued to be mined. The pit was finally closed in 1915 and the shafts sealed. All buildings on the site have been demolished, though the tunnel leading down to the abandoned Channel tunnel workings remains but locked off. Vehicle access is only through a locked tunnel where the NCB have right of access; there is, however, a steep footpath down the cliff face on to the beach. The adjacent railway tunnel is unusual in having two entrances with high and narrow pointed brick arches.

Old lighthouse, TR326418. The Roman 'Pharos' in the grounds of Dover Castle can justly be considered a piece of industrial archaeology and is one of the oldest items in the area. It probably dates from the late 1st or early 2nd century and is an octagonal tower *c*.80ft (24·4m) high with a space inside *c*.14ft (4·3m) square. The walls, of flint rubble and originally stone-faced, are set back progressively as they get higher and have recesses to carry the floor beams. It is probable that there were originally 8 storeys with a flat roof, surrounded by a parapet, on which a fire would be lighted.

Prince of Wales Pier, TR320407. This pier, built in 1893, has been recommended for listing as a Grade II structure.

Wharf crane, TR319410. On the edge of Wellington Basin, on the E side,

11 Dartford: mechanism of lock gates

there stands a 20-ton (20·4 tonnes) hand-operated crane made by the Fairbairn Engineering Co of Manchester in 1868. Not many of these are still left in the country. This one is preserved by the Dover Council (*Plate 12*). By the side of the road there is also preserved an old grappling iron used by HMS *Vindictive* in the attack on Zeebrugge Mole on 23 April 1918.

DUNGENESS

Lighthouse, TR088168. The original lighthouse tower, now disused, is brick-built 140ft (42·7m) high. Built in 1902 it ceased work in 1961 but is looked after by the lighthouse keepers and open to the public. The light was from a paraffin-vapour burner with weight-driven rotational mechanism; there were additional sector lights half way up the tower to give warning of shallows. The round house alongside, now dwellings for the lighthouse keepers, is the lower part of the original lighthouse, built in 1792 by William Coke of Holkham to the design of the architect Samuel Wyatt, which was a 120ft (36·6m) high wooden tower with a brazier on top.

EASTRY

Windmill, TR304545. A smock mill without sweeps and in poor condition. The windshaft and brake wheel still remain. Probably built in the 18th century. It lies in Mill Lane *c.*650yd (600m) W of A256.

EDENBRIDGE

Mile post, TQ445455. On W side of B2026 just S of Edenbridge. Cast-iron

12   Dover: Fairbairn crane on wharf

mile post (see EAST SUSSEX B2026 mile posts).

Windmill, TQ445455 c.½ mile (800m) S of the town. In the grounds of Windmill House just N of the hospital on the W side of B2026. The tower, without cap, is all that is left of this early 19th-century tower mill which ceased work in 1887. A few items of gearing are still left inside the building which is used as a store.

Watermill, TQ444460. In centre of town on E side of B2026 just N of bridge over R. Eden. The original mill, to the N of the present one, may date from the mid-16th century but the present mill was built about the mid 18th century with the bin floor and the lucam being added c.1900. The mill worked until 1968 when a disastrous flood resulted in fracture of the 10ft 4in (3·15m)-diameter cast-iron pit wheel. An internal breast-shot wheel 12ft (3·66m) diameter × 5ft 4in (1·62m) wide with 42 floats drove 3 pairs of stones, the 3rd having been probably added at a later date. At some time, possibly about 1900, 1 pair of stones was disconnected from the pit-wheel drive and driven electrically via bevel gears. The mill is currently being restored by local volunteers and it is hoped will be open to the public in due course.

EGERTON

Watermill, TQ915483. A 3-storey brick and timber building on the R. Great Stour c.¾ mile (1·2km) NE of the village. Now a store, the internal overshot wheel and iron pit wheel still survive. It dates from the late 19th century.

ELHAM

Old railway bridge, TR187466. A brick bridge on the disused Elham Valley Railway carrying the road from Wingmore to Bladbean over the railway c.1½ miles (2·4km) N of Elham on B2065. The parapet has rectangular panels in the outer facings. Iron girders support the roadway. The railway was built in 1887-8 and closed in 1947. There was a siding on the railway just S of the bridge.

ETCHINGHILL

Old railway tunnel, TR168395. This 100yd (90m) long tunnel on the disused Elham Valley Railway lies under the road running NE from Etchinghill to Little Shuttlesfield. It may be reached by taking a track on the left c.¼ mile (400m) SE of Etchingham on the Hythe road, descending into the cutting and walking back along the track to the tunnel entrance. The track here is much overgrown and muddy. The tunnel is of brick construction and was built by Thomas Walker c.1887. The Elham Valley Railway was closed in 1947 but much of the track is still accessible to walkers, though overgrown and muddy in places.

EYHORNE STREET

Sand pit, TQ822545. Just S of the junction of the E end of the Maidstone bypass (A20) with A2020. Sand from here was used at the Crystal Palace.

EYTHORNE

East Kent Light Railway, TR280494. This railway connected with the main Canterbury–Dover line at Shepherdswell or Sibertswold and ran to Sandwich. The disused track still exists as far as Eythorne and the start of the single-track line to Guilford Colliery at Coldred can still be seen, though the rails on this branch have been lifted. From the level crossing between Upper Eythorne and Lower Eythorne walk

W along the track; the turn-off to Guilford Colliery may be seen on the left after about 250yd (229m).

FAVERSHAM

Brewery, TR017615. Shepherd Neames brewery offices on the W side of Court Street. The firm was founded in 1698 and these buildings were erected in 2 stages, half in 1869 and half in 1900. A fine 19th-century façade.

Brewery, TR018615. Whitbreads brewery on the E side of Court Street at the N end. A fine complex of buildings in red brick and timber, built in 1764 but extensively remodelled later with mathematical tiles. The projecting, weatherboarded lucams, supported by fine decorative iron brackets, are part of the original structure.

Bridge, TR015616. This small swing bridge over Faversham Creek, between Conduit Street and Brent Hill, is a modern replacement of an earlier one but it still uses the original hydraulic accumulator and hand-operated pump of 1878 for lifting the bridge off its seatings to permit it to be swung by a wire rope and winch. The adjacent sluice gates, though not the original ones, still preserve the same manual operating mechanism, with the worm gears enclosed in the head of a mushroom-shaped pillar and the final gear operating on a rack attached to the gate.

Gun-powder mills, TR010612. Gunpowder and other explosives have been manufactured at Faversham since the end of the 16th century, the 3 principal factories being the Home Works (TR010612) established by 1653, the Oare Works (TR001622) in operation by 1719 and the Marsh Works (TR013626) opened in 1786 after the government had taken over the factories in 1760. The workshops, offices

and stores of the Marsh Works still remain, used by a gravel company who work the site. Gravel working also occupies the site of the Oare Works but the old Foreman's House, now called Davington Hill and the offices and stores still survive, together with the remains of the No 1 Magazine. The finest remains are at the Home Works where one of the chart mills has survived practically complete and is being very well restored by the Faversham Society (*Plate 13*). The 16ft 2in (4·93m) diameter breast-shot iron wheel originally operated a pair of mills, these being driven through bevel and spur gears and a large spur wheel mounted on a vertical wooden shaft, which carries the 2 edge-runner stones revolving on the bed stone. The manufacture of gunpowder was always fraught with danger and serious explosions occurred in 1767, 1781 and 1847, while a serious explosion occurred at a TNT store in 1916. A plentiful supply of water was needed, not only for driving the mills and mixing the ingredients but also for transport between the various sections in the works, which for safety reasons were well separated from one another. Banks and screen walls were also used to confine the blast effects of an explosion, and trees were extensively planted for the same reason.

Heritage Centre, TR017612. On the E side of Preston Street. An excellent display of the history of Faversham and well worth a visit. Among the industrial exhibits is an 1850 box mangle.

Old mill, TR017617. A 5-storey timber building in Denne's depot in Belvedere Road, it is built on the S edge of Faversham Creek and has a lucam overhanging the creek. Originally steam-driven and now used for storage. The best view is obtained from Front Brents on the opposite side of the creek.

Town pump, TR017614. In the Market Place at the Southern end of Court Street just North of the old Market Hall. A decorated and painted cast-iron octagonal structure *c*.8ft (2·4m) high, dating from the late 19th century.
Warehouse, TR019618. In Abbey Green on the E side of Abbey Street. A 19th-century 2-storey brick building with large entrance doors on both floors and a tiled roof hipped at both ends.
Warehouses, TR020620. On Standard Quay, a long range of 2-storey granaries possibly belonging originally to Faversham Abbey. Timber-framed with brick infilling, though the ground floor has been largely rebuilt in brick. Tiled roof with projections over 2 of the first-storey doors.

FLIMWELL

Mile post, TQ722310. A cast-iron mile post on A268, *c*.½ mile (800m) E of its crossing of A21 (see EAST SUSSEX A268 mile posts).

FOLKESTONE

Cliff railway, TR224355. An unusual, if not unique, cliff railway this is a double one, having 4 tracks and 4 cars, the first pair of tracks, built in 1885, being of 5ft 10in (1·8m) gauge, while the second pair built in 1890 are only 4ft 10in (1·5m) gauge. The railway is 180ft (54·9m) long and was originally of the water-balance type but later electrified.
Pillar box, TR216355. A free-standing Victorian pillar box at the corner of Grimstone Avenue and Sandgate Road, opposite the Metropole Hotel. On the base is the inscription 'A. Handyside & Co. Ltd. Derby & London'.
Viaduct, TR228364. A brick viaduct of

13   Faversham: gunpowder mill – note pit-wheel for drive to stones in second mill on left, now demolished

19 arches, from 40–100ft (12–30m) high, carries the South Eastern Railway across the Foord valley between Folkestone Central and Folkestone Junction. It was built in 1843 by Sir William Cubitt and is listed as a Grade II Structure.

FRITTENDEN

Watermill, TQ803417. A 3-storey brick and timber building dating from 1756. The remains of an iron overshot wheel still exist, and also some of the machinery.

GODMERSHAM

Donkey wheel, TR079505. This wheel, which may date from the 17th century, is in excellent condition and worked until 1923. It is 15ft (4·6m) diameter × 3ft (91cm) wide.

GOUDHURST

Watermill, TQ708372. Hope Mill is on the S side of A262 c.1 mile (1·6km) W of the town. Only parts of the waterwheels remain. The original wheel had a large wooden shaft with cast-iron spiders and wooden arms; a later wheel, installed at a lower level has an iron shaft, arms and rims. A few sheet-iron buckets, badly corroded, remain. The wooden bypass sluice still exists and is watertight. The wheel is preserved by the present owner who would like to restore it and use it for generating electricity for the house.

GRAVESEND

Canal bridge and lock, TQ656743. The Thames & Medway Canal terminates in Gravesend in a basin connected to the Thames Estuary by a tidal lock of which the lower gates have been removed, thus only allowing it to be used at high water. A swing bridge (one-way traffic for vehicles) crosses the lock and is operated by an endless steel cable round a drum on the bridge, passing round a pulley alongside, which is operated by a handle through bevel gears. The basin provided a very useful Marina for sailing and powered pleasure craft. See also ROCHESTER Canal basin for the other end of this canal.

Customs House, TQ652743. A square 3-storey brick building with stone cornice and string course at first floor level. An octagonal wooden lookout building stands near it on the sea front.

Old fort, TQ653743. Built in 1869 it contains 3 gun emplacements with brick arches, and an unusual open emplacement with a heavy iron shield. They are all served by underground ammunition stores. A few traces of earlier defences of 1788 survive above ground.

Pillar box, TQ657740. At the corner of St John's Road and Norfolk Road. A splendid Victorian pillar box comprising a fluted cast-iron column with a projecting top crowned by a flattish conical roof.

Railway station, TQ646740. The best frontage is the 'up' side in Rathmore Road, which comprises 2 square brick-built wings with a portico between them supported by 4 columns (now, alas, encased in wood) and 2 stone pilasters against the walls of the wings.

Royal Terrace Pier, TQ651745. Built in 1842 it has an imposing entrance flanked by 2 fine turrets housing a bell and a clock. It is T-shaped with 2 slender lantern towers at the ends and is being restored to its former excellence.

Town Pier, TQ648745. An iron structure supported on tubular columns. The wooden buildings have small square lanterns, crowned with spikes, on the 2 wings and a tall tubular column with a guiding light on it in the middle. Dating from 1834 it was used by the London, Tilbury & Southend Railway as a ferry terminus. It is now a discotheque.

Swing bridge, TQ676739. This bridge is over a section of the Thames & Medway Canal which is still in water and may be reached by following a road on the N side of the railway from Gravesend to Rochester until it crosses the canal and then a rough road on the N side of the canal. The bridge is just where the large overhead power lines come down from the N and turn E beside the canal. There is a large cast-iron counterweight on the landward N end of the bridge but there is no sign of cables or gearing for operating the bridge. As it appears to be only an accommodation bridge it was probably opened by hand.

GREAT STONAR

Railway viaduct, TR322596. The brick piers and approach embankments still remain of the viaduct built c.1916 by which the East Kent Light Railway crossed the South Eastern line from Minster to Sandwich. The bridge over the R. Stour has disappeared completely but the embankment beyond the river remains. This section of the line was closed in 1949.

GUSTON

Windmill, TR333444. c.¼ mile (400m) NE of A258 on a side road leading to the village. A tower mill without cap and not in very good condition. It was built about the mid-19th century and stopped finally c.1943 being tail-winded and damaged in 1959.

HAM STREET

Railway station, TR001337. On the Hastings–Ashford line. A good example of a SER wayside station; a 2-storey, red-brick building with yellow brick facings and stone window surrounds. It dates from c.1851.

HARRIETSHAM

Chegworth Mill, TQ850527. On the R. Len, in the village of Chegworth about 250yd (229m) S of A20 (Maidstone–Charing) on a side road to Headcorn. A 2-storey building, brick and stone, on the ground floor and weatherboarded above. Probably of late 17th century date. An iron overshot 8-armed wheel 10ft (3m) diameter by 8ft (2·4m) wide with 40 buckets is fed from the mill pond by a tunnel under the farm road. 'W. Weeks, Maidstone' on the base plate of the outboard bearing (which is missing). The cast-iron sluice and launder are in fair condition. The wheel drove 3 pairs of stones via cast-iron stone-nuts. The mill was still working in 1967 but producing animal feed only (*Arch. Cant* 1967 p 40).

HARTLEY

Disused railway station, TQ754345. Cranbrook Station, on the disused Paddock Wood–Hawkhurst line, was nearly 2 miles (3·2km) W of Cranbrook and approached by a 500yd (457m) lane from the Railway Hotel on A229. The line was completed in 1893 and used principally for the transport of hops from the hop-gardens to Paddock Wood. It was closed in 1961 and the track lifted, but the station buildings still remain, as the Cranbrook Pottery, with the station master's house as a private dwelling. The goods shed also survives.

HAWKHURST

Disused railway station, TQ757323. The terminus of the Paddock Wood–Hawkhurst line, on the W side of A229 *c*.1 mile (1·6km) N of the town. The station building has been demolished by the Kent Turnery Co, who own the site, but the platform survives and the signal box is in good repair. The goods shed, engine yard and station master's house also survive, together with a row of railway cottages on the N side.

Mile posts, TQ737308–TQ782298. Four mile posts on A268 in the Hawkhurst area, from halfway to Flimwell to halfway to Sandhurst (see EAST SUSSEX A268 mile posts).

Watermill, TQ755314. On a minor road *c*.300yd (274m) W of and parallel to A229 and *c*.½ mile (800m) N of the town. A 4-storey brick and timber building now a private dwelling. The remains of a composite overshot wheel with wooden wheel shaft still survive, together with most of the iron machinery but no stones.

HERNE

Windmill, TR185665. On a minor road *c*.½mile (800m) NE of the village. A smock mill with a high brick base dating from 1781, which stopped working in 1952. The sweeps and most of the internal machinery remain, with 3 pairs of stones. It is now being restored.

HERNE BAY

Pier, TR173683. This long pier was built 1896–9 and, unencumbered by amusement halls along its length, is a good example of a plain late Victorian pier to serve coastal pleasure steamers.

HEVER

Mile post, TQ463429. On E side of B2026. Cast-iron mile post (see EAST SUSSEX B2026 mile posts).

HYTHE

Watermill, TR166350. Built in 1773, the machinery of Hythe Mill is nearly complete, though it has not worked since the 1920s. The iron overshot wheel is 21ft 6in (6·5m) in diameter and 5ft 2in (1·57m) wide. There are 2 pairs of underdrift stone with cast-iron stone-nuts and 1 overdrift pair, probably added at a later date. Two half-shafts provide belt drives for auxiliary machines and the sack hoist is friction-driven from the top of the vertical shaft. There is also a belt-driven wire machine. The pond and bypass sluice still exist and the tail race is carried in a tunnel for *c*.300yd (275m) under the house and the road to discharge into the Royal Military Canal. A beam engine was installed in the 19th century to drive the mill but was scrapped during the last war. The mill is privately owned.

ICKHAM

Watermill, TR215581. On the R. Little Stour *c*.½ mile (800m) W of the village. Now a private dwelling but the breastshot wheel still remains though all the internal machinery has gone.

IDEN GREEN

Watermill, TQ798306. A derelict 4-storey brick and timber building dating from the early 19th century. The remains of an iron overshot wheel exist and most of the mill machinery including a very large pit wheel. Originally 4 pairs of stones. In the mid-19th century a beam engine was installed as a stand-by drive to cope with water shortages.

IWADE

Windpump, TQ913688. Just E of A249 on the approach to Kingsferry

14   Lamberhurst: well of ice-house at Scotney Castle

Bridge. A simple wooden post with 4 struts. There are 4 sweeps each made from a single piece of timber, with a wind vane at the rear. A vertical iron shaft through the framework operates a pump below; used for drainage of low-lying ground.

KENNINGTON

Watermill, TR031454. On N side of Mill Lane which runs E of A28. An early 19th century brick and tile-hung 3-storey building, now a private dwelling. The wheel and machinery have gone and the mill pond is silted up.

Windmill, TR031454. On the S side of Mill Lane opposite the water mill is the brick base of an early 19th century smock mill, now demolished.

KINGSTON

Old railway bridge, TR199510. A very fine brick-built skew bridge carry-ing the Elham Valley Railway over a lane running SW from Kingston, about halfway between Barham and Bishopsbourne.

LAMBERHURST

Ice-house, TQ689353. This ice-house is in the grounds of Scotney Castle, the gardens of which are National Trust property. It stands above the lake on the N bank, a circular thatched building. The ice well is c.12ft (3·7m) deep, 16ft (4·9m) diameter at the top and 7ft (2·1m) diameter at the bottom. It dates from 1834 (*Plate 14*).

Oast houses, TQ675355. A very fine set of 4 oast houses, dating from 1876. They are preserved externally but it is intended to convert the interiors to living accommodation (*Plate 15*).

LEEDS

Watermill, TQ823531. Only the lower

15　Lamberhurst: oast houses

storey of the Abbey Mill remains, with an internal iron overshot wheel by W. Weeks of Maidstone. 2 lay-shafts were driven by wallowers from the pit wheel with 1 pair of stones on the L.H. shaft and 2 pairs on the R.H. one.

Watermill, TQ835532. Only the walls are left of the 13th-century Castle Mill, whose breastshot wheel was fed from the moat of Leeds Castle. The remains of a pair of stones, probably 19th century, are in the bottom of the wheel pit.

LITTLESTONE-ON-SEA

Water tower, TR086252. In Madeira Road, an ornate 6-storey red brick tower with a battlemented top and buttresses at the corners. A spiral staircase in an octagonal turret at the SE corner leads up to the roof from the 4th storey. It is dated 1890 and is *c.*100ft (30m) high.

LYDD

Railway station, TR056215. This station on the Appledore–Dungeness line is a good example of a SER country station and is still complete with its buildings, platforms, goods yard and passing loop, though the tracks in the yard have been lifted.

LYDDEN

Abandoned   colliery, TR271457. Access to Stonehall Colliery is by a footbridge over the railway at the E end of the village and thence by a public footpath. A bore hole was sunk here in 1913 and 3 shafts were subsequently sunk to a maximum depth of 273ft (83m). Trouble was experienced due to the ingress of water and no coal was ever won from here; *c.*1920 the site was abandoned and the shafts sealed. The brick foundations of the head gear for 2 shafts still exist together with a derelict brick engine house (*Plate 16*).

16   Lydden: pit-head structure at Stonehall Colliery

The third shaft was to supply feed water to the boiler. The workshop buildings still remain in fairly good condition. On the hillside above are the remains of a large storage tank, with a brick-capped circular concrete wall *c.*30yd (27·5m) diameter and 20–25ft (6–7·5m) high; the wall is breached at one point.

LYMINGE

Old railway station, TR165410. On the disused Elham Valley Railway the wooden station building in the SER style is preserved and in good condition. It is used as an office for the County Council depot in the old goods yard.

MAIDSTONE

Beam engine remains, TQ756566. The beam from one of the 6 Boulton & Watt engines installed in 1805 by James Watt and John Rennie to drive Springfield paper mill, the first to be operated by steam power; it worked for 80 years. The beam, *c.*20ft (6m) long, is supported on 2 small brick pillars by the side of a pond, possibly the old cooling pond, inside the grounds of the Whatman Reeve Angel Group's works on the West side of Sandling Road.

Crisbrook Mill, TQ757537. About ¼ mile upstream from Hayle Mill, at Upper Crisbrook Mill on the R. Loose, the 16ft (4·9m) diameter × 8ft (2·45m) wide iron waterwheel has been restored. The mill is now a private dwelling. It is a 3-storey brick and timber building with double lucam, and dates from the second half of the 19th century.

Fremlin's Brewery, TQ758558. At junction of Earl Street with Fairmeadow Street. The building dates from the last quarter of the 19th century and was developed from two

small derelict breweries by the Fremlin brothers, becoming one of the largest brewing concerns in the south east. The date 1872 may be seen on the base of the fine chimney which still stands. There are some good cast-iron window frames and also cast-iron columns supporting a works bridge over Waterside, giving access to the river wharves. There is also a very fine weathervane, a gilded elephant, which was the sign of Fremlin's. The last brew took place in 1947 but parts of the site are still in use and the buildings are generally in good condition.

Fullers-earth pits, TQ7856. Fullers earth, for finishing woollen fabrics, was obtained from open-cast surface workings in the Grove Green area to the NE of Maidstone. The industry was active up to the 17th century but declined in the 18th.

Hayle Paper Mill, TQ756539. This mill, on the R. Loose, is owned by J. Barcham Green Ltd, and has a very good trade producing paper, hand made in the traditional manner. The original drive was from an iron waterwheel, 18ft (5·5m) diameter by 8ft 6in (2·6m) wide, which has provision for both pitch-back and overshot operation, the former being the normal method. It can still be run but no longer drives the machinery, the overhead shafting being now driven by an electric motor. Nearly all the old machinery still exists and much of it is in use, though the old air-drying racks and screens are no longer used. There is a beautifully made 1889 loom for weaving wire-mesh screens for the handmade paper sheets. All moulds and screens used are made on site. The old beaters are still in use and all machinery, whether in use or not, is well preserved. There is also an old National gas engine preserved and run on natural gas, and a Lancashire boiler of 1934. This is one of the few mills still left making high-grade handmade paper. There is a long tradition of paper-making among the people in the Loose valley and one of the interesting records is a set of small plaques on the wall of one of the rooms giving details of long-service employees, many of 40 and 50 years, some of 60 years and over and one, a woman, of 75 years' service. It is a great pleasure to see the old traditions of craftsmanship kept up, with many young entries, and to know that the old machines are well looked after and still in use (*Arch. Cant* 1973 p 159).

Museum, TQ759556. The Tyrwhitt-Drake Museum of Carriages in Mill Street is housed in a late 14th- or early 15th-century building, once the stables of the Archbishop's Palace. The collection comprises horse-drawn vehicles, mostly carriages and coaches, from the 18th and 19th centuries, together with some models of coaches and old bicycles and small carts. The room over the entrance porch has a wooden hand-crane and operating gears which may date from the 17th century.

Museum, TQ759560. The town museum in St Faith's Street has the iron movements of several 17th and 18th century turret clocks removed from parish churches in the neighbourhood. There are also some agricultural implements and a fine collection of old weights and measures.

Otham Paper Mill, TQ787546. On the R. Len at the junction of Spot Lane and Willington Street. These remains of an early 19th-century water-powered paper mill stand in the garden of the Mill House, whose owner is gradually uncovering and preserving them. There is a high dam to the mill pond, now silted up and overgrown, which contained the wheel-pit can be seen, which contained a waterwheel (now gone) *c*.16ft (4·9m) diameter by *c*.8ft (2·4m) wide. No machinery remains but some of the stone vats and waterways remain. This was the first paper-making mill in the Len Valley (*Arch. Cant* 1967 p 72).

Paper mill, TQ772555. Turkey Mill, the lowest mill on the R. Len, originally had 3 overshot wheels in the early 18th century. It ceased working by water in the early years of this century but is still producing a high quality paper.

Watermill, TQ757531. The ruins of Great Ivy Mill on the R. Loose still remain but the foreman's house, a fine 3-storey brick and timber building, has been preserved. The mid-19th-century iron penstock of the mill and the remains of a water turbine still exist.

Watermill, TQ802547. Thurnham Mill on the R. Len, built in the early 19th century, is now a derelict 3-storey timber building, with only the pit wheel and the remains of the iron overshot wheel left.

MARGATE

Cliff railway, TR362712. An unusual single-car railway running against the cliff face for some 70ft (21·3m) at an angle of *c*.45° from the Lower Promenade to the Cliff Top Promenade. It dates from 1912–13 and is electrically operated with iron counter-balance weights moving in a vertical shaft. The track has a 5ft (1·5m) gauge.

Pier, TR353712. This pier, built 1853–6, has been recommended for listing as a Grade II structure.

Windmill, TR362700. Drapers Mill lies just S of the road running E from the railway bridge on A255 to Northdown. Dating from *c*.1847 it has been fully restored and is open to the public.

MEOPHAM

Windmill, TQ639652. This smock mill, lying just W of A227 overlooks Meop-

17   Meopham: smock mill

ham Green. It is unusual, being a hexagonal smock mill, and was built in 1801; it ran until 1929 when an oil engine was installed in an engine house alongside to drive the machinery via belting; this was replaced by an electric motor in 1933. The mill is a small one, having 27ft (8·2m) long sails and a brake wheel of 6ft 6in (2m) diameter; it was fully restored in the early 1960s, but does not run. It is open to the public (*Plate 17*).

MERSHAM

Watermill, TR050390. On the R. East Stour just S of the village. Also known as Hanover Mill. Built in 1879 by Holman Bros, Canterbury. Although no longer used the machinery has been preserved in excellent order, behind glass screens, by the owner. There is an iron breast-shot wheel, enclosed, 12ft (3·7m) diameter by 6ft (1·8m) wide with 56 ventilated buckets. A 7ft (2·1m) diameter pit-wheel drives a horizontal shaft with spur wheels operating 2 pairs of 3ft 10in (1·17m) diameter stones, and also auxiliary machinery. On a minor road running S.W. from the village.

NEWENDEN

Mile post, TQ826278. On A268, c.330yd (300m) W of its junction with A28, a cast-iron mile post (see EAST SUSSEX, A268 mile posts).

NEW ROMNEY

Romney, Hythe & Dymchurch Light Railway, TQ074249. This railway, whose headquarters is at New Romney, though only a miniature passenger line, is now 50 years old and should rank as a piece of industrial archaeology. It was opened from New Romney to Hythe in 1927 and extended

to Dungeness by 1929. It is of 15in (38cm) gauge and all the engines were built between 1925 and 1931. Passenger carriages are some fully enclosed, some open and some semi-open.

NORTHBOURNE

Windmill, TR331521. On N side of road running SW from the village. A tall wooden smock mill dating from 1845. Although worked by wind until the 1920s and by electric drive until the 1950s it is now empty and derelict without cap or sails, though the windshaft is left.

NORTH FORELAND

Lighthouse, TR398696. The original lighthouse, built in 1636, was a wooden tower. Burnt down in 1683 it was replaced by an octagonal brick and flint tower, c.40ft (12m) high with a fire basket on top, later enclosed in a lantern. In 1793 the height was increased to c.85ft (26m) with an oil-lit lantern on top.

OARE

Windmill, TR009625. On E side of road from Faversham to Oare. A tower mill with no cap, but an octagonal pitched roof, converted to a dwelling house. The spur wheel still exists in the ceiling of one of the upper rooms. It dates from c.1900.

Windpump, TR012628. c.¼ mile (400m) NE of the tower mill at TR009625 are the remains of a small smock mill used for pumping water from the marshy ground where it now lies forlornly on its side. There were 4 spring sails and a cap on a simple wooden framework. It last worked at the end of the 19th century but was still standing, in fair condition, in 1933.

OTTERDEN

Horse-gin, TQ946542. At Otterden Place, an exceptionally fine wheel with a very large drum from which the rope extends, under a tiled roof, for *c*.17yd (15·5m) to the well head which is in a very confined space.

PENSHURST

Bridge, TQ529436. A narrow single-arched stone bridge over the R. Medway on B2176. Of 18th century date it has small octagonal piers with pointed tops at the approaches.

QUEENBOROUGH

Pier, TQ903739. This T-shaped railway pier on the SE & CR was built in 1876 to give access to deep water at the mouth of the Swale. It was closed in 1914, except for a temporary re-opening in 1923, and now only the shoreward section remains, though the foundations of the remainder can be seen at low tide.

RAINHAM

Horse-gin, TQ813645. At corner of road by Miers Court *c*.1 mile (1·6km) along lane running S from Rainham. A fine horse wheel in small building with thatched roof. A boarded drum wound up the rope over a pulley which raised a bucket from the well to fill a cistern. The horse arm has a simple claw type of clutch on the vertical shaft which engages when the horse pulls and lifts the arm. When the horse stops the arm drops, disengages the clutch and, through a pivoted arm, applies a brake to the underside of the drum. The installation is preserved by the owner.

RAMSGATE

Railway   tunnel, TR390665–TR388650. The disused railway tunnel of the SE & CR which led to Harbour Station may still be seen on the side of the road down to the harbour. The line was opened in 1863 and closed in 1926.

RECULVER

Windmill, TR224679. Chislet Mill stands *c*.¼ mile (400m) N of A299 and is reached by a side road from the Roman Galley Hotel. It is a small smock mill dating from *c*.1750 with mostly wooden machinery but no sweeps. Privately owned, it is in reasonably good condition, the body having been sheathed in corrugated iron. It ceased work in 1916, having been accidentally tail-winded.

RINGWOULD

Windmill, TR362490. Ripple Mill stands on a lane *c*.220yd (200m) W of A258 *c*.½ mile (800m) N of the village. A smock mill with no cap, sweeps or machinery, now used as a TV relay station. It dates from the early 19th century and may have been brought here from near Hawkinge.

ROCHESTER

Canal basin, TQ743694. This basin at Frindsbury marks the Medway terminus of the 7-mile (11·26km) long Thames & Medway Canal, started in 1800 and finished in 1824. At the upper end of the basin the canal entered a 2-mile (3·2km) long tunnel (now used by the railway) in the middle of which a passing place for barges was made in 1830 by opening up the tunnel at a point where the ground cover was shallow. In 1840 a single-track railway line was made through the tunnel beside the canal and by 1849 most of the canal had been filled in and a double-track line ran through the tunnel. Parts of the canal are still in water at the Gravesend end (q.v.). The tunnel entrance has a good elliptical brick arch, just beyond the N end of the basin at TQ741698.

ROLVENDEN
Post mill, TQ838315. On S side of B2086 c.½ mile (800m) W of the village. A post mill with roundhouse dating from the mid-18th century it is privately owned and was restored in 1956. Most of the machinery remains, with 2 pairs of stones and a wooden windshaft. It ceased work in the 1880s.

ST MARGARET'S AT CLIFFE

Donkey wheel, TR360451. At Townsend Farm c.300yd (274m) along a lane leading NE past the school. The 13ft (4m)-diameter wheel is in a rather confined space but is in fair condition. It is a good example of the use of a wire carried under the wheel to act as a brake.

ST MARGARET'S BAY

Windmill, TR363435. On cliff top at South Foreland. A smock mill, the youngest in Kent, being built in 1928 for generating electricity by windpower, not for milling. With patent sweeps and a fantail, it is now used for storage for the adjacent house in whose grounds it stands.

SANDHURST
Mile posts, TQ794288 & TQ808281. Cast-iron mile posts on A268 c.½ mile (800m) E and W of the village (see EAST SUSSEX A268 mile posts).

SANDLING

River lock, TQ747581. The lowest lock on the Medway, reached by a lane on the S side of A2011 just E of the Maidstone bypass. It is a double one, the upper lock being the original one built in 1791 which was extended downstream to double its length in 1883 when the pleasant stone-built lock house was erected (*Plate 18*). The operating gears for the side paddles of the upper lock are probably original. The electrically operated sluices and flood gates across the main river were installed in 1937.

SANDWICH

Toll bridge, TR332583. Built in 1773 with stone arches at the ends and the centre part probably a raised timber platform. In 1892 the centre part was replaced by an iron swing bridge.
Warehouse, TR334582. On the Quay. A yellow brick building with red brick arches dating from the mid-19th century.
Windmill, TR322586. On N side of A257 c.½ mile (800m) W of the town. A smock mill, built towards the end of the 18th century, it ran until 1953, though it was not worked by wind after 1926. Most of the machinery is intact; it was repaired in the 1960s and will be completely restored by the local council.

SARRE

Water pump, TR259650. There is an old water pump for public water supply in the garden of the Crown Hotel, in the angle between A28 and A253.
Windmill, TR259651. Just N of the village on the E side of A258. A smock mill dating from 1820, now in poor condition with no sweeps, though the windshaft and 2 pairs of stones remain. It worked by wind until 1920 when it was converted to run by steam-power.

It is hoped to restore the mill.

SEVENOAKS

Watermill, TQ536567. At Greatness on the W side of Mill Lane. A 19th-century weatherboarded building on an 18th century stone base, now an upholsterer's workshop. 6 storeys with lucam on N side. Originally an old lace mill started by Huguenot refugees, becoming a flour mill in the 19th century and later being electrically driven. Traces of the mill pond and wheel pit can still be made out.

SHEERNESS

Boathouse, TQ910753. This multi-storey ironed-framed building, erected in 1858, is one of the earliest buildings in the country to use this form of construction where the whole of the load is carried by the frame, the outer walls being merely cladding and not load-bearing structures. The frame is made of cast iron and wrought iron, the floor girders being fabricated from iron plates and angles riveted together. This is the earliest use of this type of construction in large buildings in Britain.

SHELDWICH

Toll house, TR014583. On A251 $c.\frac{3}{4}$ mile (1·2km) S of its junction with M2.

SHEPHERDSWELL

Railway station, TR258484. The station of the East Kent Light Railway built in 1912 is now used for waggon storage. The line is still used as far as Tilmanstone for transport of coal from the colliery there.

Railway tunnel, TR265488–TR269490. Golgotha Tunnel is on the

18   Sandling: lock house and lock on R. Medway

only part of the East Kent Light Railway still in operation. This leaves the main Dover line just N of Shepherdswell and serves Tilmanstone Colliery only. The tunnel has deep approach cuttings and is built for double track though only a single track was laid (*Plate 19*).

SHOREHAM

Bridge, TQ521616. 3 small stone arches over the R. Darent with a ford on the North side. The parapet on the N side is of brick and flint but that on the S side has been replaced by a modern post and rail fence. 18th–19th century, probably replacing an earlier bridge.

Watermill, TQ520622. On the R. Darent. Originally a paper mill and now a private dwelling it is an 18th-century 2-storey weatherboarded building. The mill and millhouse are under the same roof with the probable remains of an earlier structure incorporated. The waterways remain and can be traced.

SISSINGHURST

Watermill, TQ820382. The 4-storey brick and timber Hammer Mill has a composite overshot wheel and most of the machinery remains though the mill pond has been filled in. There are 3 pairs of stones.

SITTINGBOURNE

Narrow-gauge railway, TQ905642. The terminus of the Sittingbourne & Kemsley Light Railway, which operates a 2-mile (3·2km) section to Kemsley Down of the 2ft 6in (76cm) gauge system laid by the Bowater Paper Co in 1906 to connect their mills at Sittingbourne and Kemsley (TQ920664) with their dock at Ridham

19   Shepherdswell: entrance to Golgotha Hill tunnel on East Kent Light Railway

(TQ920685) on the Swale. This section, saved and operated by a preservation society, is the only part still in use and is open at weekends and on Bank Holidays, also Tuesdays, Wednesdays and Thursdays in August. Two of the locomotives date from 1905, being built to serve the original short stretch of line from Sittingbourne Mill to Lloyd's Wharf on Milton Creek, which no longer exists. Sittingbourne Mill is now supplied with high-pressure steam from Kemsley Mill through pipes running beside the railway. A unique locomotive also survives, being fireless and having a steam reservoir which was charged at 220psi from the steam mains at Kemsley Mill. It could run for about 8 hours but can no longer be used now.

SMEETH

Watermill, TR065381. Evegate Mill on the R. East Stour is a 4-storey brick and timber building, now an antique furniture repair shop. The iron overshot wheel remains and much of the machinery. Probably late 18th/early 19th century.

SOUTHBOROUGH

Brick kiln, TQ595425. This kiln, in the grounds of Forge Farm, is visible to the W of the railway about halfway between Tonbridge and Tunbridge Wells, the separate chimney being quite prominent. The arched tunnel of the kiln is now used as a cow shed. There is some dilapidation of the building, iron bands and stays having been fitted in various places.
Viaduct, TQ594429. A fine brick structure of 26 arches built in 1845 for the branch line from Tonbridge to Tunbridge Wells, now part of the main line to Hastings. c.100ft (30m) high across a deep valley.

Water tower, TQ569417. On the Broomhill Estate, now a convalescent home. A round 4-storey brick tower with a battlemented top and a small staircase turret at one corner.

SPELDHURST

Barden Mill, TQ549425. The dry mill pond can be seen on the E side of the road, where it crosses the stream on top of the dam. The mill house with prominent lucam is on the W side of the road, but it is not in good repair. Some masonry remains can be seen in the stream bank on the W side below the dam.
Watermill, TQ558417. c.¼ mile (400m) E of the village at the end of a lane leading to Bradley's (corn merchants). The wheel c.12ft (3·7m) diameter is a composite one having 8 iron arms, wooden rim and sole boards and sheet-iron buckets. It is in remarkably good condition and drives 2 pairs of stones, one of which is complete with all fittings. A 5ft (1·5m) diameter iron crown wheel with wooden cogs drives 2 layshafts with pulleys for belt-drive to sack-hoist, oat-crusher etc; there is also a pair of sack scales. The pond is in water but partly silted up and the wooden trash-rack, sluice and launder still remain. The building is in excellent condition and the owner intends to restore the mill to working order in the near future.

STALISFORD

Horse gin, TQ952552. At Wingfield Farm; an 18th-century horizontal wheel for raising water from the well by a rope and bucket. Protected by a weatherboarded structure with a corrugated iron roof.

STANFORD

Windmill, TR128379. On a lane running W from B2068 just S of the village. A brick tower mill dating from 1851, with cap but no sweeps. It worked by wind until 1946, but now stands empty in private grounds. Two pairs of stones still remain.

STELLING MINNIS

Windmill, TR146466. A tarred smock mill on a shallow brick base, it is just over 100 years old and worked until the autumn of 1970. It has now been fully restored to working order by the East Kent Mills Group and was opened to the public at the end of 1975. It stands in Mill Lane, to the S of the village.

STODMARSH

Wind pump, TR233604. ¾ mile (1·2km) E of the village, NE of the adjacent farm house, on the banks of the R. Little Stour. A simple timber post, c.12ft (3·7m) high with 4 struts. A cast-iron shaft through the post drove an Archimedean screw. Four stocks but no vanes now. In poor condition.

TENTERDEN

Mile post, TQ863333. In the centre of the town on the S side of A28 outside Webbs (ironmongers) a milestone stands on the very edge of the pavement and has so far survived destruction by heavy lorries (*Plate 20*).

Railway station, TQ882335. Tenterden Station is the headquarters of the revived Kent & East Sussex Railway which was the first line to be built under the 1896 Light Railways Act. Known originally as the Rother Valley Railway, it was opened from Robertsbridge to Rolvenden in 1900 and

20   Tenterden: milestone still standing on edge of pavement

extended to Tenterden Town in 1903 and to Headcorn in 1905, being built under the direction of Lt. Col. H.F. Stephens, its engineer and managing director for over 30 years. It was closed early in 1954. The Tenterden Railway Co, a registered charity, was formed in 1971 and early in 1974 reopened a short section of the line from Tenterden to Rolvenden. This is being gradually extended to reach its final terminus in the eastward direction at Bodiam. It is the only standard-gauge railway built to light-railway standards that is still operating in the south east and is open on Saturdays, Sundays and Bank Holidays and some Wednesdays from March to October. The oldest engine on the line, No 3, *Bodiam*, a 0-6-0 tank engine, is over 100 years old, having been built in 1872. It is a fine sight to see it puffing slowly up the 1:50 Tenterden Bank, one of the steepest

railway gradients in the south of England (*Plate 21*).

Museum, TQ882333. On W side of road to Tenterden Town Station this small museum houses a fine collection of items connected with Col. Stephens, the builder and managing director of the K & ESR. There is an extensive collection of his free passes from other railways all over the British Isles and many unique photographs of the various light railways with which he was associated. There are also some old agricultural implements and a collection of official weights and measures.

Watermill, TQ865329. Ashbourne Mill is an 18th-century 3-storey brick and timber building with lucam. The overshot wheel has been replaced by a turbine but most of the internal machinery remains with 2 pairs of stones, a governor and various auxiliary machines. The mill lies just N of A28 close

21   Tenterden: 100-year-old locomotive *Bodiam* on 1:50 Tenterden Bank

to the level crossing on the Kent & East Sussex Railway, West of Tenterden.

TILMANSTONE

Colliery, TR289506. This colliery, started in 1906, is still in full operation after overcoming considerable trouble with water ingress when sinking the shafts to a depth of c.3000ft (914m). Two shafts with modern headgear are working but adjacent to the No 1 shaft is the original engine house which houses a mobile winder, used in emergency with the original headgear at the top of an early shaft which goes down to the 1500ft (457m) level. Three of the original workshops and the original offices are still in use.

TONBRIDGE

Museum, TQ590467. The SE Electricity Board have established the 'Milne Museum' in The Slade, Castle Street, Tonbridge, which houses a fine display of early electrical distribution equipment and domestic electrical appliances, some of the latter being of a very early date and most interesting. A decorated cast iron distribution pillar, of an early date, is one of the last surviving ones in the region. Apply to SEEBOARD for access.

WEST KINGSDOWN

Windmill, TQ582623. On the SW side of A20 just SE of the village. An early 19th century smock mill, originally at Farningham and moved to its present position in 1880 at a cost of £80. The machinery is largely intact with 3 pairs of stones, but with no quants or casings. The original fantail was unusual in having 7 blades, but it has now been replaced by a 6-bladed one. The mill is well cared for and the sweeps were due

to be replaced in 1976–7.

WESTWELL

Watermill, TQ992474. A 4-storey brick and timber building, now a private dwelling. The iron overshot wheel remains, partly derelict. Late 19th century.

WHITSTABLE

Old Customs House, TR109670. An attractive 2-storey brick building with a hipped, tiled roof, and a decorative cornice below the 1st-floor windows.
Old railway bridge, TR115665. The remains of one of the oldest railway bridges in the world, as the Canterbury–Whitstable Railway was opened in 1830, the same year as the Liverpool–Manchester Railway. All that is left of the bridge are the approach embankments and the brick abutments.
Toll house, TR105656. On a triangular island in the middle of a road junction. A single-storey brick building with slate roof and tiled ridges. There is a projecting bay with observation windows and what is probably a toll hatch.
Windmill, TR106652. Just E of A290 at the approach to the town. An early 19th-century smock mill, the base and 1st floor are occupied by the Windmill Motel, but the upper floors still retain most of the original machinery including a wooden wallower. It is hoped to restore it to working order in the future.

WICKHAMBREUX

Watermill, TR220586. On the R. Little Stour, on the edge of the village. No longer in use but the fine breast-shot wheel may be examined; 17ft (5·2m) in diameter there are a few paddles left and some gearing. An early 19th-century mill.

WILLESBOROUGH

Windmill, TR032422. On Mill Lane between A292 and A20 to the E of Ashford. A large smock mill on a 2-storey brick base, it dates from 1869 and worked until 1938 when an electric drive was installed and ran until 1969. The main internal machinery, with 4 pairs of stones, is intact but the sweeps and fantail are missing. It is in urgent need of repair and a fund has been opened for the restoration of the mill.

WITTERSHAM

Windmill, TQ913273. Stocks Mill stands c.1 mile (1·6km) E of the village at a crossroads where B2082 turns S. A post mill with roundhouse, it is the tallest of the post mills in Kent and has 4 sweeps with spring sails. The roundhouse is now a garden store, but carved on the centre post are the dates 1781, 1785 and 1790 with the initials of the contemporary millers. Though on private ground, it may be inspected by interested visitors. It is in good repair.

WOODCHURCH

Windmill, TQ943352. c.1 mile (1·6km) N of B2067 just E of a minor road to Bethesden. A smock mill on a tall brick base, it dates from c.1820, and has 4 stocks but no sweeps or fantail. The internal machinery and 3 pairs of stones are intact. It belongs to the parish and although scheduled as an Ancient Monument it is badly in need of repair.

WYE

Ice-house, TR062486. On E side of road opposite Olantigh Towers just S of side road at top of hill. Of brick with an arched entrance partly destroyed. The ice-well itself is filled with rubbish.

Watermill, TR049468. On the R. Great Stour. Now used as a store, the 3-storey brick and timber building contains an iron undershot wheel and fine sluice gates but no machinery. Mid-19th century.

Surrey

Two waterways of particular interest to industrial archaeologists exist in Surrey, the Basingstoke Canal linking London with Basingstoke and the Wey & Arun Canal which, with the Wey Navigation, afforded a direct water route from London to the south coast. The Basingstoke Canal, which leaves the Wey Navigation c.1100yd (1km) above New Haw Lock, runs due W and crosses over into Hampshire at Aldershot. It rises 185ft (56·4m) in 16 miles (25·7km) through 28 locks, c.75ft (22·8m) × 13ft (4m), these being mainly concentrated in flights of 13 at Pirbright, 6 at Woodham and 5 at Woking. It crosses the main railway line by an aquaduct at Mytchett near Frimley and, with a further single lock just over the county boundary, it enters the 21-mile (33·8km) level stretch to Basingstoke. Started in 1788 it was opened throughout in 1794 and reached its peak traffic in 1838. Abandoned in the early part of the 20th century it is now being restored by a voluntary preservation society. The troubled history of the Basingstoke Canal and its railway competitor is fully set out in P.A.L. Vine's *London's Lost Route to Basingstoke*.

The Wey Navigation is an early one, the river having been made navigable to Guildford in 1653 and extended to Godalming in 1763; it is still open, mainly for pleasure craft, under the ownership of the National Trust. The Wey & Arun Canal leaves the Wey Navigation at Shalford and rises 48ft (14·6m) in 5 miles (8km) through 7 locks to its 5-mile (8km) long summit level at Cranleigh. It then falls 53ft (16·2m) in 1 mile (1·6m) to its entry into W Sussex near Loxwood (for further details see under WEST SUSSEX). The summit level is fed from Vachery Pond, S of Cranleigh, c.1½ miles away to the E and, between 1833 and 1834, 2 windmills were installed adjacent to the locks at Cranleigh and Birtley to pump water up from the lower reaches to the summit level, thus making the canal one of the very few in the country to employ wind-power for pumping. The windmills ran until 1853 when they were scrapped and the equipment sold off; nothing now remains of them.

ADDLESTONE

Coxes Lock, TQ061641. The lock is beside the Allied Mills Ltd works. Though nothing is left of the old watermill there is a water turbine still working to supply power to the Allied Mills plant. The main office building dates from the 18th century and the building housing the turbine is older.

ALBURY

Chilworth Mills, TQ025475. Gunpowder mills had existed at the little village of Chilworth since c.1625, and by the late 19th century had become one of the most important in the country. The mills were originally driven by waterwheels on the R. Tillingbourne, which also supplied power for paper mills. A millstone from the gunpowder works still remains half-buried on the site, and a pair of cottages, believed early 17th century, were once included in the grounds of the works.

ALFOLD

Wind pump, TQ053345. At Pallinghurst Farm a ruinous wind pump, dating from c.1910, used for water-raising for the farm buildings.

ASHTEAD

Ice house, TQ193583. The ice house for Ashtead House, now in the Farm Nurseries on Farm Lane. 18th century, with a stepped entrance to a domed brick building c.10ft (3m) in diameter with an iron grating floor.

BETCHWORTH

Lime kilns, TQ208514. c.300yd W of B2032. Turn off in Betchworth village just over ½ mile (800m) N of the junction with A25. The chimney can

be seen from a considerable distance. There are very extensive chalk quarries in the escarpment of the North Downs with the remains of the old railway tracks in them. Two lines of kilns remain, one partly ruinous surmounted by 2 tall brick-built flues, the other with 4 circular brick-built charging towers, in fairly good condition. There is also a very tall brick-built double kiln with a split flue, standing alone (*Plate 22*). The old Pilgrim's Way passes above the kilns and below the largest quarry, which has completely eaten away the end of a ridge.

BRAMLEY

Birtley Wharf, TQ018435. The N end of a stretch of the Wey & Arun Canal still in water. Below Waverley D.C. Depot, just across the disused Guildford–Horsham Railway. The track of

22 Betchworth: charging towers of lime kilns in foreground, double kiln with split flue in background

the old railway may be followed on foot for a considerable distance S from here.

Gosden Aquaduct, TQ007456. A public footpath runs along the dry canal bed and the aquaduct (*Plate 23*), over a tributary of the Wey, lies just beside the remains of a skew railway bridge over the same stream. At TQ006457 a typical canal bridge has been incorporated complete into a later road bridge which crosses the canal and railway together.

BROCKHAM

Village pump, TQ197495. At Brockham Green, on the green in the centre of the village. A 19th-century cast-iron pump inside a wooden casing, under an ornamental wooden structure with a tiled roof, surmounted by a small wooden cross.

BROOKWOOD

Canal locks, SU955571–SU958571. A flight of 3 locks on the Basingstoke Canal lifts the water level 20ft (6m) in c.350yd (107m).

BUSBRIDGE

Water tower, SU987428. On the SE side of a side road to Munstead Heath, c.550yd (500m) NE of B2130. A fine late 19th-century octagonal brick tower, c.100ft (30m) high, with a stair turret on the upper part of the E side leading to the tank and parapeted roof.

CHARLWOOD

Windmill remains, TQ245409. The octagonal brick base of a smock mill has been converted into a private house. It dates from c.1800 and lies on a side road just S of the village.

23   Bramley: Gosden Aquaduct on the Wey & Arun Canal

CHIDDINGFOLD

Windmill remains, SU952339. Only the octagonal brick base of a smock mill, dating from 1813, is left standing in a field on the W side of S283, about 1 mile (1·6km) S of the village. It has a pyramidal roof and is used as a store. Known as 'Hungry Corner Mill'.

CLAYGATE

Telegraph tower, TQ158647. One of the chain of Admiralty semaphore stations for relaying messages between London and Portsmouth. Semaphore House, a 3-storey tower with a flat roof.

COBHAM

Bridge, TQ092605. An 18th-century road bridge carrying A3 over the R. Mole. Built in 1783, and widened on the N side in 1914, it is a fine brick structure of 9 arches, the river flowing through the central ones. There are 2 pedestrian recesses on each side of the roadway.

Mile posts, TQ118616. On Fairmile Common on A3 on the N side of the road, c.100yd (91m) S W of the junction with Fairmile Lane, there is an old milestone incorporated into a chain fence. It is c.18in (46cm) square and 3ft (91cm) high, set square to the road. Although very eroded the markings 'Esher 2, Cobham 1' can be made out, but the distances to London and Portsmouth are now illegible. On the S side of the road, c.25yd SW of Fairmile Lane is another milestone, similar to that at ESHER (TQ127629), marked 'Esher 2, Cobham 1' on the sides, 'Hyde Park Corner 16' on the front and 'Portsmouth 53' on the top. It is obviously of the same series as the one at ESHER, but the first mentioned one is of a different series. Another mile post, of the same type, can be seen on the S

side of A3 at TQ105605, nearly opposite the police station; the top is illegible, the front is marked 'Hyde Park Corner 17' and the sides 'Esher 3' and 'Ripley 4' (see ESHER, RIPLEY and SEND for further milestones in this series).

CRANLEIGH

Elm Bridge Wharf, TQ039390. On the Wey & Arun Canal where B2130 (Cranleigh-Godalming) crosses the canal. The N. section of the canal has been partially cleared but the S. section is still overgrown and silted up. Both sections are in water though the bridge blocks the canal to navigation, there being only a culvert beneath it. The wharf is on the summit level of the canal.

DORKING

Town pump, TQ165494. On NW side of South Street, just before its junction with West Street. A 19th-century rectangular cast-iron pillar surmounted by a decorative cast-iron guide post.

Watermill, TQ180502. Old Castle Mill on the R. Mole, on the N side of A25 below the Watermill Restaurant, just E of which a public footpath leads down to the mill. An early 19th-century brick and timber 4-storey building with slated Mansard roof, now a private dwelling. The iron breast-shot wheel remains and there are some old sheet-iron paddles and wooden starts on the bank of the head-race. Some new wooden paddles have been fitted.

Watermill, TQ173506. Pixham Mill, on the SW side of Pixham Lane. A 3-storey brick building with weatherboarded gable. Early 19th century, now a private dwelling but the waterways still remain.

EAST CLANDON

Ice-house, TQ068519. On National Trust property at Hatchlands, situated among trees on a hill to the SE of the house. A very fine small ice-house with domed roof and arched entrance passage, with decorated arched doorway. The ice-well is floored over at the level of the entrance (*Plate 24*). Open Wednesday and Saturday afternoons in the summer, from 2 p.m. to 5.30 p.m.

EAST MOLESEY

Bridge, TQ153682. On Hampton Court Way over the R. Ember. Designed by Sir Edwin Lutyens *c.*1930, it has a single concrete arch with red facing bricks and a central shield with a coat of arms.

EDENBRIDGE

Watermill, TQ419455. Haxted Mill on the R. Eden, is *c.*700yd (640m) beyond Haxted on a side road running W from Edenbridge and just in Surrey. It has been fully restored to working order and is a live museum of milling, with many machines and other devices relating to water-milling and water-pumping. There is a good display of drawings, illustrations and old postcards of mills and milling processes. In the bin floor under the roof is an interesting exhibition of the Wealden iron industry, with samples of slag and ore, diagrams, and a slide show and recorded talk. The oldest mill in Surrey, the W half of the building dates from *c.*1680, being built on the foundations of the original 14th-century mill; the E half was built in 1797. The mill, with 3 pairs of stones, worked for 250 years until 1949 when grinding ceased. The waterwheel is 9ft (2·74m) diameter × 9ft (2·74m) wide and is *c.*140 years old, although the buckets were

24 East Clandon: ice-house at Hatchlands

25   Edenbridge: Haxted watermill; buckets are only fitted to centre third of wheel

replaced with fibre-glass ones in 1968 (*Plate 25*). As well as a working model of a watermill there is a Ruston & Hornsby 1920 hot-bulb oil engine and a Crossley 1913 gas engine. Scheduled as an Ancient Monument.

ESHER

Mile post, TQ147655. On the corner of the road outside the Orleans Arms. This is an exceptionally fine one in the shape of a stone cylinder *c.*3ft (91cm) diameter and 6ft (1·82m) high standing on a 2ft- (61cm) high plinth and with a stone ball on top. On different sides are marked the distances to various places up to Hyde Park Corner and West-minster Bridge in one direction, Ports-mouth in another direction and Hampton Court and Walton-on-Thames in a 3rd direction (*Plate 26*).

Mile post, TQ142640. In Milbourne Lane, between houses Nos 24 and 26. The stone is *c.*18in (46cm) square and 3ft (91cm) high, and is marked on the front face 'XVII miles from the Standard in Cornhill, London'.

Mile post, TQ134630. In a private housing estate in Claremont Park. This stone, *c.*18in (46cm) square and 3ft (91cm) high, is very well preserved and set in a surround of flint cobbles beside a footpath. It is marked on three sides as follows:

'XVI miles III Quarters from
Westminster Bridge, 1768'
'XVIII miles from the Standard in
Cornhill, London, 1747'
'XVII miles II Furlongs VIII
Poles from Newcastle House by
Hyde Park Corner' (*Plate 27*)

26   Esher: mile post outside the Orleans Arms

27   Esher: milestone in Claremont Park

The problem of these milestones between Esher and Cobham is interesting. This one and the one in Milbourne Lane (TQ142640) are obviously of the same series, and probably also the one on the N side of the road at Fairmile Common, COBHAM (TQ118616), although this does not have Roman numerals on it. The ones in Claremont Park and Milbourne Road are at approximately the correct distance from the one on Fairmile Cobham but are not on the direct A3 road through Esher but set on side roads or paths to the SE of it. *Plate 28* shows the relative positions and the relevant roads. It seems probable that the two milestones now in Claremont Park and Milbourne Lane originally stood on the main A3 road, the former at TQ127629 and the latter at approx. TQ136642 (where there is now no stone) and were moved to their present positions when road widening or building operations necessitated their removal.

Mile post, TQ127629. Set in the S side of the cutting on A3 just SW of Claremont House. The stone is square, set diagonally to the road with a bevelled top and the front corner cut away. It is marked on the sides 'Esher 1, Cobham 2', on the front 'Hyde Park Corner 15', on the top 'Portsmouth 54'. It is much eroded, particularly on the front and top, but still quite legible (see COBHAM, RIPLEY and SEND for further milestones in this series).

Tollhouse, TQ145654. On the N side of A3 opposite Littleworth Common Lane. It is a long building, the W end of it may be the original toll cottage. An old cylindrical boundary stone *c.*2ft (61cm) diameter and 3ft (91cm) high is set into the wall of the house but, being cement-rendered any inscription on it can no longer be read. Adjacent to it is a coal-tax post.

EWELL

Mile post, TQ219627. A square milestone just N of the entrance to Bourne Park; marked '4 Miles to London'.

Railway station, TQ215627. Ewell West Station in Chessington Road dates from *c.*1847. A charming small country station and almost unchanged. It is brick-built, of 2 storeys, with 2 gables; the R.H. half is the Station Master's house. The platform canopy, supported on iron columns, is original and the waiting room on the opposite platform has decorative iron brackets to support its canopy.

Watermill, TQ219631. Upper Mill, on W side of Kingston Road, is a 4-storey, 3 bay brick and timber building with wide gables over the bays and a 2-storey lucam on the N side of the centre bay.

Water wheel, TQ219628. In NW corner of grounds of Bourne Park. A 19th-century iron undershot wheel with sheet-iron paddles, *c.*7ft (2m) diameter, it is mounted under a flint-built arch with a sculptured mask on the keystone and statues on either side. It originally drove a pump for supplying water to the house.

EWHURST

Windmill, TQ077426. *c.*1½ miles (2·4km) NW of the village, on a hill in the grounds of a private house. A 4-storey brick tower mill, built *c.*1840 it ceased work in 1885 and was converted to a private dwelling in 1901; it has an ogee cap and 4 patent sails. At a height above sea level of *c.*800ft (224m) it is probably the highest mill in the county. It is difficult to find as it is nearly hidden by the trees which have grown up all round it.

FARNHAM

Farm buildings, SU832467. At junc-

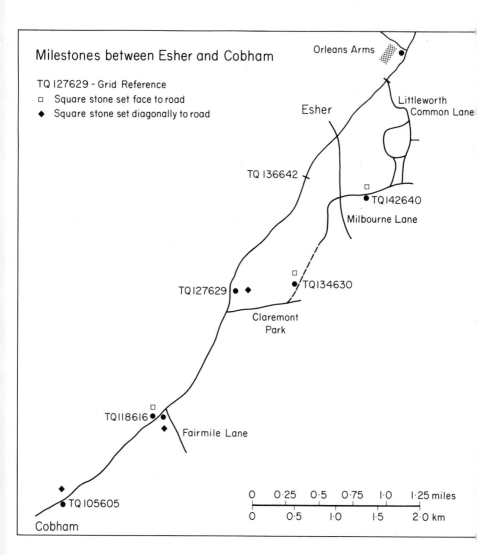

Milestones between Esher and Cobham

TQ 127629 - Grid Reference
□ Square stone set face to road
◆ Square stone set diagonally to road

Orleans Arms

Esher

Littleworth
Common Lane

TQ 136642

TQ142640

Milbourne Lane

TQ127629

TQ134630

Claremont
Park

TQ118616

Fairmile Lane

TQ 105605

Cobham

| 0 | 0·25 | 0·5 | 0·75 | 1·0 | 1·25 miles |

| 0 | 0·5 | 1·0 | 1·5 | 2·0 km |

28 Map showing milestones at Esher

tion of Beavers Road and Crondall Lane. A mid-19th-century iron-stone and brick building with tiled roof; 2 storeys with a hoist for the granary on the upper floor. The brick cottages opposite were originally the drying kilns.

Lamp posts, SU839471. About 18 tall Victorian lamp posts on both sides of Castle Street. Originally gas-lit but now converted to electricity. 3 further lamp posts may be seen in the churchyard on the S side of West Street at SU839468.

Mile post, SU841470. At the corner of Bear Lane on the N side of East Street; a square pillar set diagonally to the road at the edge of the pavement. The top is marked 'Farnham' and the front 'London 38'. On the L.H. side is 'Basingstoke 12' on the front and 'Winton 26' on the back. The R.H. side is marked 'Alton 9' on the front and 'London 38' on the back.

Old lamps, SU838468. Outside No 15 West Street over the entrance to a passage leading to the churchyard on the S side of the street. A very fine ornamental wrought-iron structure spanning the passage and supporting a lamp. A similar one, on a smaller scale, may be seen over the gate into the churchyard from Vicarage Lane at SU839469 beside a tall Victorian lamp post.

Watermill, SU858471. High Mill at the N side of Moor Park Lane. An 18th-century weatherboarded building with a half-hipped Mansard tiled roof. The mill is a 2-storey building, as is the brick and tile-hung millhouse alongside. Some machinery still remains.

Watermill, SU852474. Bourne Mill, just W of the roundabout on Guildford Road at the start of the Farnham Bypass. A 17th- and 18th-century building, partly altered in the 19th century, and now an antique shop. A fine 3- and 4-storey block, the lower floor being in brick and the upper floors part tile-hung and part weatherboarded. It dates from the period when Farnham was a great corn market for the South of England.

FELBRIDGE

Mile post, TQ371402. One of the 'Bowbells' series. On A22 c.½ mile (800m) N of the junction with A264 (see EAST SUSSEX A22 Mile posts).

FRIMLEY

Windmill, SU896563. The lower 3 storeys of a brick tower mill have been furnished with a conical tiled roof and were incorporated into a large private house in 1914. It dates from the end of the 18th century and lies just S of A231 at Frimley Green.

GODALMING

Old factory, SU982444. Just over ½m (800m) N of Godalming Bridge over the R. Wey on A3100 turn right, cross the river and the factory is on the left. The works are marked 'J.I. Blackburn & Co., Engineers & Founders, Cattershall Works, Godalming', and are partly derelict, the remainder being used for light-engineering constructions. Mechanical power was obtained from a large vertical-shaft, Fourneyron water turbine, with 100in (2·54m) diameter intake and c.6ft (1·83m) head. This still exists, though not used, and appears to be in good condition as it is completely submerged in the tail race and the shaft and gears above water level are well greased. The makers are Macadam of Belfast. Some of the shafting still remains, including some large gear wheels up to 12ft (3·66m) diameter. There is also a very large lathe which was driven from the turbine by belt-drive from overhead shafting. The lathe is of the gapped-bed type, 25ft (7·6m) long and can take work pieces of 3ft (91cm) diameter by 15ft (4·6m) long, or 5ft (1·5m) diameter by 1ft (30cm) long in the gap. It is in fairly good condition. There are tentative proposals to turn part of the works into an industrial museum and preserve both the turbine and the lathe.

Water tower, SU969447. On Frith Hill above the town to the NE a fine tall brick water tower, still in use, with a covered reservoir alongside (*Plate 29*).

GODSTONE

Mile post, TQ350521. On E side of A22 just S of its junction with A25 from Oxted, *c*.3ft (91cm) high × 18in (46cm) square, set against a wall. Although worn, the following inscriptions can be made out or deduced:

N side: 'XX miles from the Standard in Cornhill London 1744' (*Plate 30*)
W side: 'XIX miles from Westminster Bridge'
S side: 'XX miles from the Standard in Cornhill'

The E side is not visible as it is set close up against a wall.

GOMSHALL

Ice-house, TQ105472. On a low hill just to the S of the Abinger Hall water pump. In good condition but the well is blocked with rubbish. Brick-built with a short straight arched entrance passage.

Lime kiln, TQ115484. About 250–300yd (229–274m) E of the minor road running N to Effingham just after it

29   Godalming: water tower

crosses the Dorking–Guildford railway line. An unusual concrete lime kiln built to a French design between the wars (1918–39), using methods novel to this country. It failed and the company was wound up and abandoned. The kiln consists of a rectangular concrete structure with 2 through tunnels, each fed from above through a hopper with sides formed by a sloping grid of iron bars. An unusual relic.

Water pump at Abinger Hall, TQ105473. On the Tillingbourne Stream. An iron breast-shot wheel 10ft (3m) diameter by 10in (25cm) wide, driven from the stream, operates a 3-throw pump by means of beams. The pump draws water from a 40ft (12·2m) deep well in the chalk and delivers water over *c.*800yd (731m) to a 30,000 gallon (136,380 litre) tank supplying

cottages and outbuildings. It dates from 1868 and probably replaced a 2-throw pump dating from 1803 or earlier. The wheel may well be the original one which drove the 2-throw pump. The pump is still run regularly, but it is on strictly private ground.

GUILDFORD

Telegraph tower, TQ002492. Early 19th century. One of the chain of Admiralty semaphore stations relaying messages between London and Portsmouth. On Pewley Hill, a cement-rendered 2-storey building with a 3-storey square tower. The tile-hung octagonal turret with leaded domed roof was added after the station was closed.

Warehouses, SU992497. A fine range of 3- and 4-storey warehouses on the

30 Godstone: milestone

banks of the R. Wey.

Watermill, su996492. In Millbrook, now the workshops of the Yvonne Arnaud Theatre. An 18th-century 3-storey brick building with hipped tiled roof and tile-hung gable ends. A later extension to the W is dated 1896.

Wooden crane, su994495. A splendid 18th-century slewing wooden crane on the quayside at Guildford, on the E side of the R. Wey, opposite the bus station. The motive power was a large treadmill 20ft (6·1m) diameter by 4ft (1·22m) wide, housed in a wooden building alongside, with a chain to the hoisting hook. The whole installation is in good condition being preserved by the town and in the charge of Guildford Museum (*Plate 31*). Last used in 1908.

HASLEMERE

Museum, su907332. This interesting little educational museum has several items of industrial archaeological interest. There is a toll board from Winterton Tollgate at Chiddingfold, dating from *c.*1824, giving tolls for steam vehicles and dog-drawn vehicles as well as the more usual items. In the historical section there are agricultural and domestic tools and appliances from the 18th and 19th centuries and an exhibition showing the development of the timber-framed cottage. The Wealden iron industry exhibition includes a model of a Sussex Weald iron foundry of 1600, details of the last furnace built in Sussex in 1776 at Furnace Pond, Fernhurst, and a 19th-century blacksmith's forge with examples of blacksmith's work. There are a number of cast-iron firebacks of 1582, and one with the arms of the Clothworkers' Company, possibly locally made, dated 1659, with the initials W.V. on it. There is also an

31   Guildford: wooden crane on wharf; tread mill is in house on right-hand side

exhibition of Wealden glass-making.

HURST GREEN

Watermill, TQ397506. Coltsford Mill just off Mill Lane, c.1½ miles (2·4km) S of Oxted, on the upper reaches of the R. Eden with a large mill pond having a circular overflow weir. The building, which dates from c.1830, is of brick below and timber-framed above; the mill house is now a restaurant but the mill itself is a working mill and grinds regularly. An iron waterwheel 16ft (4·9m) diameter × 4ft (1·2m) wide with a 10ft- (3m)-diameter pit wheel, also of iron with wooden cogs, drives 4 pairs of stones. The spur wheel is 9ft (2·7m) diameter and the crown wheel 6ft (1·8m) diameter; 3 of the pairs of stones are complete with their fittings and there are also a dressing machine, a winnowing machine, a smutter and sack scales. There is also an old electrical generator by Laurence Scott of Norwich, 145 volts DC, 25amp, 875rpm, which can be driven from the mill machinery and is used to light the building in case of power failures.

KINGSWOOD

Windmill remains, TQ258548. Mugswell Mill. The circular brick roundhouse is all that is left of this post mill, built in the first quarter of the 19th century. It has a conical roof and is used as a garden store for the mill house. At the junction of Monkswell Lane and Green Lane.

LEATHERHEAD

Horse-gin, TQ185558. The octagonal weatherboarded wheel-house, dating from c.1800 remains, but without any gearing. Originally used for water-pumping.

LINGFIELD

Mile post, TQ364432. One of the 'Bow Bells' series. On A22 c.½ mile (800m) N of the crossing of B2028 at New Chapel (see EAST SUSSEX A22 Mile posts).

MERSTHAM

Iron rails, TQ290542. About 12 cast-iron rails from the old Surrey Iron Railway are preserved on the E side of A23, S of B2031. The Jolliffe Arms is just N of this. They are angle section, about 2ft 6in (76cm) long, slightly higher in the centre of their length than at the ends, and are laid on stone sleepers.
Railway bridge, TQ288558. A brick single-arch bridge over the track of the old Surrey Iron Railway, where the road to Netherne Hospital crosses it. The arch can be seen on the N side but is blocked on the S side where the track has been filled in and a garden constructed.

MICKLEHAM

Bridge, TQ170537. A fine 3-arched brick bridge over the R. Mole, with cutwaters and wrought-iron railings. The large centre arch has 3 keystones, the centre one being adorned with sculptured masks at each end; the smaller side arches have 1 keystone. 18th/19th century construction.
Bridge, TQ169543. A 4-arched 19th-century brick bridge over the R. Mole, with cutwaters and brick parapet.
Farm buildings, TQ169541. A fine range of farm buildings at the Priory; brick and flint barns with hipped, tiled toofs.
Ice-house, TQ174527. In the grounds of the Field Study Centre at Juniper Hall, on the S side of the road to Headley. c.25ft (7·6m) long, 10ft (3m)

wide and 10ft (3m) deep, it is in good condition.

MYTCHETT

Aquaduct, SU893565. Close to Frimley Green the Basingstoke Canal takes a sharp turn to the S and crosses over the main London–Southampton railway. The aquaduct was originally built by the L & SWR in 1838, when the line was constructed, as a double-track one and was 134ft (41m) long with 2 arches. In 1900 the aquaduct was rebuilt by the railway company when the tracks were increased to 4 and, to avoid closing the canal and incurring heavy damages, it was rebuilt to double its original width so that one half could be in use while the other half was being rebuilt (*Plate 32*).

OCKHAM

Telegraph tower, TQ089585. The old Admiralty Telegraph tower on top of Chatley Heath. A track up the hill from the E passes close by it on the S side. The tower is 60ft 6in (18·4m) high, octagonal, built of brick and 5 storeys high. It was finished in 1823 and last used in 1848, for passing messages between London and Portsmouth, being a link between the lower towers at Telegraph Lane, Claygate and Pewley Hill, Guildford. It is the only 5-storey tower still standing. Now empty and closed, but parts of the original signalling equipment are preserved at the Historic Buildings and Antiquities Office, at County Hall, Kingston. The tower is scheduled as an Ancient Monument and is protected.

OCKLEY

Windmill remains, TQ147395. Built in c.1803, the octagonal brick base of a

32 Mytchett: aquaduct taking Wey & Arun Canal over London–Southampton line

smock mill is all that is left of a mill which collapsed in 1944. Roofed with corrugated iron and standing in a field on the E side of A29, it is now used as a farm store.

OUTWOOD

Post mill, TQ328455. One of the finest post mills in the south of England. Built in 1665 it is the 4th oldest mill in the country and the oldest one still working. There is a tradition that people watched the Great Fire of London from the top of the mill not long after its construction. Repairs and replacements will of course often have been carried out since then and the present oak crown tree is dated to 1880. The cross beam above the quarter bars of the trestle, which are mounted on 5ft- (1·5m)-high brick plinths, is however said to be the original one. The brick roundhouse, 22ft (6·7m) internal diameter, was probably added after the mill was built. The mill has patent sweeps, controlled by elliptical springs; it is open to the public at the weekends and grinds flour occasionally (*Plate 33*).

PIRBRIGHT

Canal locks, SU943569–SU911565. Between Brookwood and the entrance to the 1000yd- (914m)-long cutting at Deepcut the Basingstoke Canal rises 95ft (29m) in 2 miles (3·2km) through 14 locks. Extensive restoration work is now in hand on these. For the whole of this stretch it is parallelled by the main London–Southampton line and the L & SWR, when building the line, was compelled to erect a high brick wall whenever the tracks were within 100ft (30·5m) of the canal and on the same level or below it to prevent frightening the barge-horses on the towpath. A good view of part of this wall may be obtained from Curzon Bridge, SU921564.

PYRFORD

Newark Mill, TQ040574. On the Wey Navigation where it is crossed by B367. The mill has gone but the wheel-pits can be seen. There is an old warehouse on the bank of the stream, brick-built with timber inserts. Late 18th century. By the side of the weir about 120yd (110m) N there is a bronze plaque to commemorate the flood-control measures carried out between 1912 and 1928, with the aid of much voluntary labour. Newark Lock is about 300yd (274m) downstream. **Walsham Lock,** TQ578050. This is a flood-lock on the Wey Navigation, both gates being normally open except at times of flood. It is one of the very few turf-sided locks left and also has the distinction of being one of the few locks with peg-and-hole paddles on the gates, the paddles being raised by hand and kept in position by a peg slipped through a hole in a vertical iron bar projecting up from the top of the paddle (*Plate 34*). There is another example of these at Worsfold Gates Lock at SEND. The lock is in very good condition being in regular use. There is an old weir on the main river, with 4 gates, built by Jesse Stone in 1884, and a newer one alongside built by Ransome & Rapier in 1931. The towpath changes sides here and the horse crossed by the bridge over the weir. The boat was then warped out of the lock by a cable passed round a pulley, which may still be seen.

REIGATE

Flanchford Watermill, TQ235479. A large mill pond just E of the R. Mole beside Flanchford Bridge, *c.*2 miles (3·2km) SW of Reigate. The mill is

33 Outwood: post mill, the oldest mill still working

preserved and, having a large slow-running waterwheel 20ft (6·1m) diameter × 5ft (1·5m) wide, has an additional pair of spur gears of 3:1 ratio between the waterwheel and the pit-wheel to give the necessary increase in speed; even so, both the pit-wheel and great spur-wheel are 8ft (2·44m) diameter. There are 2 pairs of stones and a small wire machine for cleaning and grading the meal.

Reigate Heath Mill, TQ234501. On the golf course behind the club house. A post mill of 1765 with roundhouse. The mill stopped working c.1870 and in 1880 the roundhouse was converted into a chapel, and is still used as such. The body and sails are fixed and in addition to the tail pole there is a fantail mounted halfway down the rear of the body. This is a very curious place to find it as it could not possibly have worked efficiently mounted where it is.

The mill was restored in 1964 and is maintained by Reigate Council. It is scheduled as a Building of Historic Interest.

Wray Common Mill, TQ269511. A tower mill about 750yd (729m) E of A242. Brick-built in 1824, with a nice ogee cap. Common sails but one sweep is missing. The fan tail exists but has one blade missing. The mill ceased work c.1895 and is now part of a private residence. It has cast-iron, Gothic-type window frames and a Palladian-type doorcase. The mill is scheduled as a Building of Historic Interest.

RIPLEY

Mile posts, on the S side of A3, 2 further milestones of the same type as at Esher and Cobham. At TQ058570 just before the sign 'Ripley' E of the village, marked 'Portsmouth 48, Hyde

34   Pyrford: Walsham lock on Wey Navigation; note turf sides to chamber and peg-and-hole paddles on gates

Park Corner 21, Cobham 4 miles, Guildford 6 miles'. At TQ045561, marked 'Portsmouth 47, Hyde Park Corner 22, Ripley 1, Guildford 5'. All the remaining milestones between Cobham and Ripley have been lost due to road widening. See COBHAM, ESHER and SEND for further milestones in this series. Also at TQ066578 is a much weathered boundary stone between Ockham and Wisley parishes, on the S side of the slip road to Ripley.

Ockham Mill, TQ056579. At Ockham Court. A fine 4-storey brick building, with brick decoration on the walls and round windows and doors. The date '1862' is on the front of the building; the adjacent mill house is of the same date. No waterwheel or machinery is left, only the intake sluice dated '1841'. There is a 2-storey wooden lucam on the gable end in front. The buildings are privately owned and are in very good condition.

RUDGWICK

Railway station, TQ076351. Baynards Station on the abandoned Christs Hospital–Guildford line is still complete with goods shed and station nameboard. A handsome red-brick, 2-storey building, now a private dwelling, with an elegant platform canopy supported on central iron columns. The station was sited to serve Baynards Park and is well away from any village as Rudgwick had its own station, now demolished (*Plate 35*).

RUNFOLD

Drying kilns, SU868484. At Badshot Lea Farm on St George's Road. A 19th-century brick building with 4 slatted and tile-roofed vents.
Drying kilns, SU871478. Hewett's Kilns, on Tongham Road. An L-shaped building of clunch and brick

35   Rudgwick: Baynards Station on disused Horsham–Guildford line

with ironstone and rubble and a half-hipped roof. 3 parallel ranges of kilns in the EW wing and 1 range in the NS wing.

SEND

Mile posts, of the same type as those at ESHER, COBHAM and RIPLEY. At Burnt Common TQ037547, on the S side of A3, marked 'Portsmouth 46, Hyde Park Corner 23, Ripley 2, Guildford 4'. At Nuthill Farm TQ027535, on the N side of A3, marked 'Portsmouth 45, Hyde Park Corner 24, Ripley 3, Guildford 3'.

Worsfold Gates Lock, TQ016557. On the Wey Navigation. Although the lock gates were replaced in 1969 the old peg-and-hole paddles are still preserved (see PYRFORD (Walsham Lock) for a description of these).

SHALFORD

Watermill, TQ001476. National Trust property on the R. Tillingbourne, dating from the first half of the 18th century. Brick ground floor with 2 timber-framed storeys above. Internal breast-shot wheel of iron with wooden paddles, c.12ft (3·7m) diameter × 8ft (2·4m) wide driving 3 pairs of stones. The mill has been fully restored and both it and the mill house, which is privately occupied, are in excellent condition. Part open during daylight hours by application.

Stonebridge Wharf, SU998464. Just N of Stone Bridge on A281 where it crosses the Wey & Arun Canal. This was the terminal wharf of the canal where it joins the Wey Navigation. Now it is just a green bank beside the canal, with houseboats moored there. The track of the disused Guildford–Horsham Railway can be seen 100yd (91m) to the S.

SHAMLEY GREEN

Run Common Wharf, TQ033419. On the Wey & Arun Canal where the road from Cranleigh to Bramley crosses it. The canal has been cleared for a few 100yd to the S where there is a winding hole. It is blocked at opposite ends by the road and by the disused Guildford–Horsham railway c.½ mile (800m) to the S. The N section is being cleared.

TADWORTH

Windmill, TQ236553. At the N end of Banstead Heath. A post mill of c.1750 with an unusual 2-storey round house, the lower part of brick, the upper of wood. It ceased work in 1890 and is now partly ruinous in the body and with no sails.

THAMES DITTON

Water tower, bridge etc, TQ163673. At the corner of Summers Road, opposite Thames Ditton Island, beside Ye Olde Swan public house is an old water tower on the wall of a private house. The suspension bridge across to the island was put up in 1939. Beyond the inn there is an old bronze foundry which is due for demolition. A travelling gantry crane from this has been rescued and is now in store pending re-erection by the industrial archaeology section of the Surrey Archaeological Society when a suitable home can be found for it.

TILFORD

Museum, SU859434. A private collection of farm implements and machinery, including a complete wheelwright's shop. c.¾ mile (1·2km) W of Tilford, between Tilford and Millbridge.

WALTON-ON-THAMES

Bridge and Tollhouse, TQ093665. The brick-built arched approaches and parapets of the first toll bridge, built in 1759, still remain, spanned by the iron truss girders of the later bridge, which replaced it in 1863–4, supported by 3 brick pillars on the original stone bases in the river. This bridge is still in use as a footbridge alongside the modern road bridge. On the old Middlesex bank on the S side of the road can be seen the toll house of brick and tile, contemporary with the toll bridge.

WEST HORSLEY

Drinking trough, TQ079523. A marble water trough, dating from 1909, erected by the 'Metropolitan Drinking Fountain & Cattle Trough Association'.
Pumping station, TQ079523. A 19th-century pumping station of the Woking Water & Gas Co. Brick-built with cast-iron, round-headed windows. The elegant brick chimney for the original steam engine still stands, though overgrown with ivy.

WEYBRIDGE

Bridge, TQ069647. Where Addlestone Road crosses the R. Wey, just beside Town Lock. This is an old 3-arched iron-girder bridge with fine cast-iron railings. The first cut on the Wey Navigation starts here and rejoins the river at Walsham Lock, PYRFORD (TQ578050).
Lock, TQ073655. *c.*100yd (91·4m) below Thames Lock, the lowest lock on the R. Wey, there is a single wide-beam wooden gate, designed to raise the water level upstream of it to give 3ft (91cm) depth over the bottom sill of the lock.

WHITELEY

Village, SU094625. Built by the millionaire William Whiteley in 1907 for 350 elderly employees. The central part is in the form of an octagon with 8 avenues radiating from a central monument.

WOKING

Canal locks, SU980580–SU986582. Here the Basingstoke Canal rises 33ft (10m) in *c.*½ mile (800m) through a flight of 5 locks.

WOODHAM

Canal locks, TQ033610–TQ051619. Past Woodham the Basingstoke Canal rises 37ft (11·3m) in *c.*1¼ miles (2km) in a series of 6 locks.
Scotland Bridge & Lock, TQ046615. An elliptical single-arched bridge over the Basingstoke Canal where B367 crosses it. The lock upstream is very decrepit though the upper gate still holds water.

East Sussex

Apart from the Wealden iron industry which has few field remains above ground, though a number have been excavated, East Sussex is largely an agricultural county and its industrial archaeology consists mainly of rural industries, transport and some light industries in Brighton.

There is only one canal in the county, the Royal Military Canal, the major part of which is in Kent. Built in 1806 as a defensive measure against Napoleon's threatened invasion, it had only a limited commercial use and is now an amenity water, though not navigable throughout. Its defensive nature is shown by the zig-zag bend every 600yd (549m) or so which allowed enfilading fire to cover the sections between the bends.

The only navigable rivers are the Ouse and the Eastern Rother. The Ouse, which enters the sea at Newhaven, was made navigable for barges in 1812 for a distance of 30 miles from the sea, to Upper Rylands Bridge, TQ325280, near Balcombe Viaduct in W Sussex. The Upper Ouse Navigation, above Lewes, was finally killed by the railways, c.1870, but the Lower Ouse Navigation, from Newhaven to Lewes, is still navigable by barges and pleasure craft.

The Eastern Rother, much of which is in Kent and which flows out at Rye Harbour, was navigable by sailing barges up to Newenden, TQ836270, until the 1930s, but is now given over to drainage. Some buildings still remain at Maytham Wharf, TQ868276, where a World War II pill-box has been constructed inside a small warehouse.

Railway remains are many, though tending to disappear before British Rail's bulldozers, and the 18th century Turnpike roads have bequeathed a number of toll houses, mostly converted to other uses, and several long and exceptionally interesting series of mile posts (*Plate 36*).

A 22 MILE POSTS

The longest continuous series of mile posts is on A22, and stretches from Lingfield (Surrey) to Hailsham. Although 2 of these are in Surrey and 4 at East Grinstead are now in West Sussex, the majority are in East Sussex and, for reasons of continuity, they are all treated together here. The Turnpike Trusts involved were the City of London–East Grinstead (1711) extended to Wych Cross by 1785, the Malling Street–Wych Cross (1725) and the Union Point to Langney Bridge (1754). All the mile posts are of cast iron and are of the 'Bow Bells' type (*Plate 37*), so called from the string of 5 bells below a bow of ribbon; above the bow is a large dot but between Uckfield (44 miles) and Horsebridge (54 miles) the dot is replaced by the Pelham Buckle, the crest of the Pelham family who were large landowners along the route of the turnpike. The distances from London, miles, location and map references are as follows:

Distance	Location	Map Reference	Distance	Location	Map Reference
26	Lingfield (Surrey)	TQ 364432	39	Fairwarp	TQ 451262
			40	Maresfield	TQ 460254
27		Missing	41	Maresfield	TQ 466241
28	Felbridge (Surrey)	TQ 371402	42	Uckfield	TQ 476227
			43	Uckfield	TQ 472210
29	E Grinstead (W Sussex)	TQ 381391	44	Uckfield	TQ 480198
			45	Framfield	TQ 489184
30	E Grinstead (W Sussex)	TQ 395382	46	Halland	TQ 495175
			47	Halland	TQ 505165
31	E Grinstead (W Sussex)	TQ 406377	48	E Hoathly	TQ 522164
			49	E Hoathly	TQ 518150
32	Ashurstwood (W Sussex)	TQ 419364	50	Whitesmith	TQ 527140
			51	Golden Cross	TQ 534126
33	Forest Row	TQ 426353			
34	Forest Row	TQ 421339	52	Lower Dicker	TQ 550119
35	Wych Cross	TQ 419325			
35	Wych Cross	TQ 422316	53	Lower Dicker	TQ 564114
36	Chelwood Gate	TQ 434305	54	Horsebridge	TQ 579113
37	Chelwood Gate	TQ 441291	55	Hailsham	TQ 590097
			56	Hailsham	TQ 586084
38	Nutley	TQ 442277			

36   Map showing turnpikes and mile posts in East Sussex

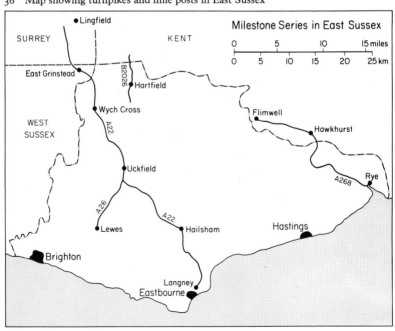

The posts at 33 and 47 miles are replacements erected in 1957 and the one at 55 miles is a 1973 replacement. Between Hailsham and Langney along B2104 the original posts were missing but were replaced in 1973; their locations are:

Distance	Location	Map Reference
57	Hailsham	TQ 590069
58	Stone Cross	TQ 604062
59	Stone Cross	TQ 613049
60	Friday Street	TQ 622037
61	Langney	TQ 630024

The reason for the duplicate post at 35 miles is that in the early 19th century road improvements in Surrey added $c.\frac{1}{2}$ mile (800m) to the road so all the posts to the S had to be shifted. The Wych Cross trustees refused to shift their post at 35 miles so a new post had to be erected $c.\frac{1}{2}$ mile (800m) N of this. This has a poor imitation of the Pelham Buckle on it.

A 26 MILEPOSTS

A further series of 'Bow Bell' mile posts, but without the Pelham Buckle exists on A26 between Uckfield and Lewes, their location being:

Distance	Location	Map Reference
44	Uckfield	TQ 475193
45	Little Horsted	TQ 468182
46	Isfield	TQ 462168
47	Isfield	TQ 450156
48	Barcombe	TQ 442141
49	Ringmer	TQ 434128
50	Lewes	TQ 425116

The one at 48 miles is a replacement of 1970

A 268 MILEPOSTS

A series of cast-iron plates on stone pillars exists on A268 between Flimwell (Kent) and Rye. Here also they are all treated together, although nearly half of them are in Kent. The Turnpike Trust involved is the Flimwell (Kent)–Rye (1762). Their locations are:

Distance	Location	Map Reference
45	Flimwell (Kent)	TQ 722310
46	Hawkhurst (Kent)	TQ 737308
47	Hawkhurst (Kent)	TQ 753308
48	Hawkhurst (Kent)	TQ 765304
49	Hawkhurst (Kent)	TQ 782298
50	Sandhurst (Kent)	TQ 794288
51	Sandhurst (Kent)	TQ 808281
52	Newenden (Kent)	TQ 826278
53	Northiam	TQ 836270
54	Northiam	TQ 829256
55	Northiam	TQ 830243
56	Beckley	TQ 843237
57	Beckley	TQ 857241
58	Beckley	TQ 869235
59	Peasmarsh	TQ 884230
60	Peasmarsh	TQ 896225
61	Playden	TQ 912226
62	Rye	TQ 921214

Replacement iron plates were fitted to the posts at 45 and 54 miles in 1974, the plate at 47 miles is still missing. The ones at 49 and 51 miles have old replacement iron plates.

B 2026 MILEPOSTS

A further partial series of plain iron posts exists on B2026 from Crockham Hill (Kent) to Duddleswell in Ashdown Forest, the route of the Wester-

37   Bowbells milestone at Golden Cross. Note Pelham buckle at top

ham and Edenbridge Trust (1767).

Distance	Location	Map Reference
24	Crockham Hill (Kent)	TQ 442503
27	Edenbridge (Kent)	TQ 445455
29	Hever (Kent)	TQ 462429
31	Cowden	TQ 474399
32	Cowden	TQ 481386
33	Hartfield	TQ 480368
34	Hartfield	TQ 480308
35	Hartfield	TQ 478338
36	Hartfield	TQ 471324
37	Duddleswell	TQ 469310

The post at 33 miles is a 1974 replacement. All distances given above are mileage from London. (*SIH* No 5 Winter 1972/73 p 2 and No 7 Spring 1976 p 23)

ALCISTON

Tithe barn, TQ505055. A fine old tithe barn, built of flint with a steeply pitched tiled roof at Alciston Court. There are 2 sets of double doors, one with a gabled porch over it, and an extension at right angles at one end. It originally belonged to Battle Abbey.

ASHBURNHAM

Brick works, TQ684161. On N side of minor road from Penhurst to Ponts Green. Part of the industrial complex of the Ashburnham Estate. A double kiln, the covered firing area and outbuildings still remain. The last wood-fired kiln in Sussex, it finally ceased work in 1968 (*SIH* No 1 Winter 1970/71 p 2).
Iron furnace, TQ685170. On track N from Ashburnham Forge on Penhurst–Ponts Green road, 17th to 18th century. The last iron furnace to be worked in Sussex, it was finally blown out *c*.1820.

The masonry wheel-pit still remains though much overgrown, one of the few stone relics of this industry in Sussex.

ASHBURNHAM-BATTLE

Mile posts, TQ704148–724171. Late 18th century. Three identical stone mile posts on the line of a disused private carriage road from Ashburnham Place to the Flimwell–Hastings turnpike. They are of sandstone 3ft 7in (1·1m) high and are set at TQ704148, 716157 and 724171. The last of the 3, marked '55 miles from London – 2 miles to Ashburnham Place', is on a bank beside the old coach road, now a forest track (*SIH* No 5 Winter 1972/73, op. cit.).

BARCOMBE

Horse-gin, TQ418143. At Court Lodge Farm. A circular, open-sided horse-gin house, beside the approach to the church. It has a thatched roof supported on timbers. No machinery left.

BARCOMBE CROSS

Disused railway station, TQ417158. The single-platform Barcombe station lies on the NE side of the old railway. The approach is just beyond the over-bridge opposite the road sign 'Barcombe'. The buildings are of brick, single storey with a tiled roof, the station master's house having an upper tile-hung storey. The platform canopy is gone and the buildings are slowly decaying. To the left of the station entrance door are 2 panels reading 'L.B. & S.C.R.' and the date '1882'; there are also incised flower designs on plaster similar to those in W Sussex at COCKING and SINGLETON. There is an Edward VII letter box on the corner of the road bridge.

BARCOMBE MILLS

Locks, TQ433148. On Upper Ouse Navigation. The upper and lower lock chambers still exist above and below Pikes Bridge, on the bridle road approach to Barcombe House. The site of the old mill is not at all obvious. The locks are now used as weirs, and the navigation is a fish ladder.

Railway station, TQ429149. On Lewes–Uckfield line. Main buildings are in fair condition and the station master's house is occupied. Cast-iron columns support the platform canopy. Track lifted but crossing gates remain. A notice states that the footpath beside track can be used by the public when road is flooded. Unusually long platform. Victorian postbox in wall of building.

BATTLE

Hospital, TQ731159. The Battle Cottage Hospital is unusual in having been originally a workhouse, as its appearance and plan plainly show.

Railway station, TQ755155. Designed by William Tress for the SER in 1852. A fine example of a Victorian country roadside station (*Plate 38*). Externally it is unaltered except for the chimneys. The roof, baronial fireplace and Gothic doorway to the booking hall are all worth seeing. The platform canopy is later and overshadows the 5 sandstone arches opening on to the platform.

Toll house, TQ738160. On S side of A269. A two-roomed cottage with tiled roof extended on the W side with matching brickwork. Built in 1766 on the Battle–Broyle Park Gate turnpike. Note the small observation windows on the sides (*Plate 39*).

Windmill, TQ747166. Between A21 and B2092 N of Battle. A small mill, built in 1810 by William Neve replacing an earlier post mill. Cased in zinc

38   Battle: railway station

sheeting in 1894, a new cap and stocks were fitted in 1970. Now a dwelling house.

BEAUPORT PARK

Farm museum, TQ785156. At Norton's Farm there is an interesting small display of old agricultural machines and implements, including a Sussex farm waggon still in use.

BERWICK

Brickworks, TQ527075. On W side of B2108, ½ mile (800m) N of Berwick Station, opposite the car park for Arlington Reservoir. Derelict remains of an old brick and tile works. A brick ramp leads to the top of the pug-mill house which contains 'Berry's Patent Brick Machine' electrically driven via belting. There are 6 tunnel driers, c.40yd (36·6m) long × 4ft (1·2m) wide

× 5ft (1·5m) high. The walls of 3 kilns still exist, c.28ft (8·5m) × 12ft (3·7m) × 11ft (3·3m) high. These were fired from outside, there being 10 openings per side. Owned by the Firle Estate.

BOARSHEAD

Blacksmith's shop, TQ535326. c.¼ mile (400m) beyond the Boar's Head Inn, on the E side of A26. The smith, Mr J. Fenner, now 90, is possibly the last maker of hand-made edge-tools left in England. He developed and made the first non-magnetic steel tools used in defusing magnetic mines in the last war. There is a very fine collection of blacksmith's tools, mostly made by Mr Fenner himself, and an old brick tyring furnace behind the workshop. The forge has been worked by Mr Fenner's father and grandfather before him and is believed to date from c.1720.

39 Battle: Toll house; note observation window on side

BODIAM

Railway station, TQ782250. This will be the terminal station of the Kent & E Sussex Railway, when the reconstruction of this is completed. A pleasant little weatherboarded building, typical of the ones on this light railway (*Plate 40*).

Watermill, TQ783267. On W side of road from Staplecross to Bodiam, on the Kent Ditch which forms the Kent/Sussex boundary. Only the wood and iron waterwheel is left, in rather poor condition.

BREDE

Toll house, TQ826183. On E side of A28 in the middle of Brede village, almost opposite the church. It has a mansard tiled roof and is believed to be 18th century.

Water-pumping station, TQ814178. Reached by a lane leading W from A28 just before the top of Brede Hill. Owned by the Southern Water Authority, it supplies water to Hastings and the surrounding district. A fine Edwardian industrial building dating from 1903, which originally housed two 410HP Tangye triple-expansion steam engines (*Plate 41*) pumping water from 275ft- (83·2m)-deep wells and delivering it through triple ram force pumps to a height of 515ft (157m) to reservoirs above Hastings. The engines were installed in 1904; one has been sold for scrap but the other is still kept for emergency standby, using Babcock & Wilcox boilers installed in 1939 and 1948. It is hoped that this engine can be preserved. There is also a 420HP Worthington Simpson triple-expansion engine in another building installed in 1941, making it probably the last one of its type to be installed in the country.

40 Bodiam: station on Kent & East Sussex Railway

Coal for the station was originally taken by barge from Rye up the R. Brede to the road bridge at TQ827175 and thence by an 18in- (46cm)-gauge light railway to the station. The route of this can be traced fairly easily and some wooden sleepers still remain half-buried in a cart track.

BRIGHTLING

Horse-gin, TQ686206. A square house on the W side of a cartshed, open on one side. No machinery is left.

Watermill, TQ686201. A water-driven saw mill on the Brightling Park Estate. A fine example of late Victorian workshop construction, being built about the turn of the century. The 16ft (4·9m) diameter overshot composite waterwheel by Neve is dated 1891, and the date 1902 is cut on the brickwork inside. The wheel no longer works and the saw bench is driven by a tractor

when necessary. On private land. It is hoped to restore this to working order. It has now been listed as a Grade II building.

Watermill, TQ696199. All that is left of Darwell Mill is a weir and some masonry in the stream in the middle of a wood.

BRIGHTON

Brewery, TQ316049. In Waterloo Street, Tamplin's Phoenix Brewery extends over several acres. The nucleus of it, rebuilt in the late 19th century, is at the north end of Albion Street.

Coachworks, TQ316041. In Chapel Street. Workshops and stables dating from the 1820s, on 3 sides of a courtyard with the entrance between 2 tall stuccoed brick walls, which were designed to hide the works as it lies directly behind St George's Church. No machinery is left and the building

41 Brede: pumping-engine house

is at present occupied by a metal company.

Foundry, TQ316041. In Chapel Street, Kemp Town. Known as Palmer's Foundry, it dates from the 1820s. Only a small site, it is concealed behind a 60ft (18·29m) frontage. There is no machinery left.

Intercepting sewer, TQ314037. In the mid 19th century all Brighton's sewers discharged straight into the sea, if not actually on to the beach. After a long and often acrimonious battle an intercepting sewer was built along the front from the boundary with Hove to Portobello just E of Peacehaven where an outfall extended well out to sea. It was designed and built by Hawksmoor, the railway engineer, 1871–4 and collects the output of the Hove sewer, 2 main sewers down London Road and Lewes Road and several smaller ones. Of ample proportions for future needs, the brick work is superb and in excellent condition after more than 100 years of service. Arrangements can be made with the Southern Water Authority for parties to visit it at low spring tides, i.e. on summer evenings about twice a month, a visit which is well worth while.

Malthouse, TQ313045. In Cheltenham Place. Two rows of 8 windows down Blenheim Place still have their original grills. The kiln and the maltsters' room are later.

Palace Pier, TQ314037. Built 1898–9, it has an extraordinary mixture of styles. It is already listed as a Grade II structure and has been recommended for raising to Grade II Star.

West Pier, TQ303037. This is 1863–6. It is unfortunately damaged and is now closed to the public as being dangerous. It is already listed as a Grade II structure and has been recommended for raising to Grade I, but the cost of repairing it and preserving it is estimated to be very high indeed.

Railway bridge, TQ308053. A large cast-iron bridge carrying the LB & SCR over New England Road. Built by Regent Foundry, Brighton, it is a rare type as cast-iron bridges were later banned by Act of Parliament, owing to the weakness of cast iron under tensile stress. Many were replaced by steel, but this one has had inverted RSJs fitted to strengthen it.

Railway station, TQ310049. Built by David Mocatta in 1840. The original façade has been nearly hidden by the late Victorian canopy over the forecourt. The train-shed canopies, installed in 1883, are a remarkably fine example of cast-iron construction over a curved track. Unfortunately they break the skyline of the Mocatta building. British Rail wish to demolish and rebuild the station, but the train sheds should be preserved at the very least, if the Mocatta building cannot be.

Railway viaduct, TQ309056. A beautiful curved brick-arched viaduct carrying the Brighton–Lewes line over London Road. There are 26 semi-circular arches with a central elliptical arch 67ft (20·4m) above the roadway. Built by Raistrick in 1864, his typical hollow piers are visible from the road beneath.

Rottingdean Railway, from TQ335033 westwards. Only visible at low tide, the lines of concrete blocks about 100yd (91·4m) out are the sleepers for the 'Daddy Long Legs Railway in the Sea'. The 2 tracks of 2ft 8½in (83cm) gauge were 18ft (5·5m) apart. An overhead electric supply powered motors which drove down the legs to the wheels. It ran from the Banjo Groyne to Rottingdean under the official name of the 'Brighton & Rottingdean Electric Tramway'. Begun in 1894 it was opened in 1896 and ran until 1901 when the lengthening of various groynes caused its closure.

Volk's Electric Railway, TQ316038–

332035. The first public electric railway in Britain, it is still operating. It runs along Brighton front from the Aquarium to Black Rock, $c.1\frac{1}{4}$ miles (2km). Opened by Magnus Volk in 1883 it was extended to Paston Place in 1884 and to Black Rock in 1901. Of 2ft 9in (84cm) gauge, a 3rd rail supply was installed $c.$1893. Much of the permanent way and the Paston and Black Rock stations were replaced 1947–8, but most of the cars, though often rebuilt, date from 1897–1901. The present Aquarium Station is a former tramway shelter.

A number of old warehouses, dating from the first half of the 19th century existed recently. Though used for different purposes, they are mostly 2- and 3-storey buildings though a few are of 5 and 6 storeys. They may be found in Upper Gardner St (TQ312045), Gloucester St (TQ312047 and TQ314047), Queen's Place (TQ314050), Bond St (TQ311043), Station St (TQ311048) and Black Lion St (TQ310039). They are, however, fast disappearing as development proceeds. **Several small 19th-century workshops** can also be found, mostly in the eastern parts towards Kemp Town. Some are purpose-built, others of a conventional type mostly of 2 or 3 storeys, and none of the original machinery remains. They may be found at Dorset Mews (TQ315042), Bloomsbury St (TQ325038), Chapel St (TQ327038) and Eastern Rd (TQ322041), where there is also the original 'Albion Steam Flour Mills' with an imposing tower.

BROAD OAK

Iron-making site, TQ836212. Beckley Furnace, dating from 1650, was at one end of a long bay $c.$10ft (3m) high with a forge and boring mill at the other end $c.$170yd (155m) away. The bay is breached at the S end by the R. Tillingham and a timber structure, probably part of the wheel-pit, can be seen in the stream bed. In the millhouse garden there is a cast-iron slab $c.$4ft (1·2m) long. At a later date the pond was drained and a leat run from the river higher up to supply a corn mill.

BURWASH

Iron graveslab, TQ677247. A badly defaced cast-iron slab on the wall of the church, in memory of Jhone Colins. Because the style of lettering is said to be Lombardic, it has been claimed that this shows it dates from the 14th century, but cast iron was not made in Sussex until $c.$1497, and grave slabs and fire-backs were not produced until $c.$1550.

Watermill, TQ677238. Dudwell Mill. The sluice is all that remains of this, though a mill is known to have existed here in 1347, and was possibly built 100 years earlier.

Watermill, TQ671236. Park Mill, on the R. Dudwell, is on the Batemans Estate, owned by the National Trust. It is a 3-storey brick and timber building dating from 1750 and has lain empty and unused since 1903 when Kipling removed the waterwheel and installed a water turbine to drive a generator which supplied light to the house until the 1920s, after which time the generator and turbine also were left unused. Between 1970 and 1975 the mill was restored to working order by the Sussex Industrial Archaeology Society and the turbine and generator fully repaired and restored by instructors and students of the Mechanical Wing of the Royal School of Military Engineering at Chatham. A new waterwheel was built, of half the original width owing to the turbine penstock and drain tube occupying half of the width of the wheel-pit (*Plate 42*). The turbine is by Gilbert Gilkes, Kendal (1903), of Vortex type and 4HP, 280rpm, the generator by Cromptons, 105˚/150˚, 15amp, 1000rpm and the switchboard by Christy Bros & Middleton, Chelmsford, all of *c*.1903. Entry is through the gardens at Batemans House, open March–October, every day except Fridays (*SIH* No 7 Spring 1976 p 7 and p 13).

BURWASH COMMON

Watermill remains, TQ656225. At Willingford Farm, on S side of road from Burwash Weald to Brightling. The dam and tail race of a medieval watermill (*c*.1314), belonging at that time to Robertsbridge Abbey, can still be traced about 100yd (92m) inside the field gate leading to the farm.

BUXTED

Watermill, TQ494235. A 19th-century slate building which is a dwelling house. Interior has been completely gutted but the cast-iron overshot wheel, *c*.9ft (2·7m) diameter, remains.

CADE STREET

Toll house, TQ606210. On B2096, the Heathfield–Battle road, this small originally 2-roomed brick cottage has been absorbed into a much larger house. It was built in 1813.

CATSFIELD

Water tower and pump, TQ711151. A brick water tower, with 36,000 gallon (164,000 litre) tank on top and 140ft-(43m)-deep well alongside. It supplied Normanhurst, the home of Lord Brassey, now demolished. The original 3-throw pump at bottom of well, and the drive to it from a steam engine at base of tower, still remain though the engine has gone. At a later date a large

42 Burwash: Park Mill, Batemans; waterwheel, launder and control sluice

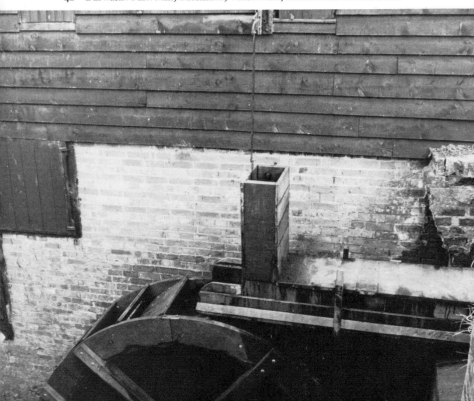

single-cylinder pump was installed at the bottom of the well. This was driven from an oil engine which still remains. This pump has been removed though the A-frame and gearing for it still remain.

CHAILEY

Windmill, TQ387214. On N side of A272 at North Common. A 19th-century smock mill with brick base and 4 sweeps. No machinery left. Built originally at W Hoathly in 1830, it was moved to Newhaven in 1844, and to Chailey in 1864.

COLEMAN'S HATCH

Newbridge Furnace, TQ456324. All that is left of the oldest iron furnace in Sussex is the dam, now breached, and the spillway. The first mention of the furnace is at the end of the 15th century.
Watermill, TQ456328. The 18th/19th-century Newbridge Mill, a picturesque weatherboarded structure now used as a dwelling house. The basic machinery, however, remains, including parts of the iron overshot wheel, *c*.10ft (3m) diameter. The stones have gone.

COWDEN

Iron furnace (Scarletts), TQ443401. The furnace is on the S side of a minor road from Cowden to East Grinstead and is right on the boundary between Kent and East Sussex. It dates from the time of the Commonwealth and has been excavated by the present owner who hopes to preserve it. The wheel-pit for the furnace bellows has been uncovered and the furnace itself has been excavated. A gun-casting pit has also been exposed. Two leats at different levels have been exposed in the dam, possibly for small water-wheels.

CRIPPS CORNER

Road bridge, TQ776212. This small bridge carries B2089 over A229, the Hastings–Hawkhurst turnpike, which dates from *c*.1841 and was the last turnpike to be built in Sussex. The narrow arched bridge is of ashlar with modern iron railings and is the last fly-over of this type left in Sussex since a similar one carrying A2100 over A21 at Baldslow (TQ798132), was demolished for road widening in 1973–4.

CROSS-IN-HAND

Windmill, TQ557218. On a side road between A267 and A265. A 19th-century post mill with roundhouse. With an iron windshaft and wooden brake-wheel it originally drove 2 pairs of stones (underdrift) from a spur wheel; only 1 pair is now left. A pair was also driven from the tail wheel. It worked until 1970 when the sweeps were damaged in a gale. It is now being restored. Built originally at Mt Ephraim, Framfield in 1806, it was moved to Cross-in-Hand in 1855 and erected 500yd (457m) SW of its present position, to which it was moved in 1868. The largest post mill in Sussex.

DALLINGTON

Watermill, TQ652201. Cox's Mill, *c*.½ mile (800m) N of B2096 down a narrow lane. The building, now used as a summer house and store, and the mill pond remain. Of the machinery only the sack hoist and the waterwheel bearing remain.

DANE HILL

Watermill, TQ416257. Sheffield Mill is a small brick and timber building, unused but still cared for. It is interesting in having a wooden layshaft drive to 2 pairs of stones mounted on a separate hursting. The cast-iron overshot wheel, 14ft (4·3m) diameter, is by Medhurst and is dated 1869 though the mill itself dates from the 18th century. The mill pond is an old hammer pond for a furnace, to which the name, Furner's Green, of the neighbouring hamlet seems to bear witness.

DITCHLING

Lamp standards, TQ324151–329155. A fine series of Victorian lamp standards has been preserved in this village, and has been augmented by a group formerly at Lewes Station installed by the LB & SCR in 1889. They have been converted from gas to electricity using new lamps designed in the traditional style.

EASTBOURNE

Pier, TV618989. The pier dates from 1872. The concert hall and pavilion were added in 1888. It is listed as a Grade II structure and has been recommended for raising to Grade II Star.

EAST DEAN

Belle Tout Lighthouse, TQ563955. On the coast road between Birling Gap and Beachy Head stands Stephenson's granite lighthouse of 1831. The lantern is gone and it is now a dwelling house. Mist and low cloud frequently obscured the light, leading to its abandonment and the construction of the present lighthouse at the foot of Beachy Head.

ETCHINGHAM

Railway station, TQ714263. Built of ragstone by William Tress in the Tudor style, it is one of the pleasantest station buildings between Tunbridge Wells and Hastings. Erected by the SER between 1851 and 1852.

EWHURST

Water pump, TQ786237. At Prawl's Farm there is an old water pump dating from c.1925. A single-cylinder pump in a well reputed to be 400ft (122m) deep, the headgear is unusual in that it contains a counterweight, connected by chains and pulleys to the top of the pump rod, which is necessary to balance the weight of the very long rod to the pump at the bottom of the well. It was originally driven by a small petrol engine which also drove a dynamo for battery charging. The pump is no longer used and it is hoped it may be possible to transfer it later to an open-air industrial museum to be established at AMBERLEY in W Sussex.

Oast house, TQ786237. On Prawl's Farm, an oast house complete with drying floor. There is no circular passage with firing holes to the central chamber which appears to have been fired directly from outside.

FOREST ROW

Watermill, TQ416353. The 19th-century watermill of Brambletye House was demolished in 1968–9. The mill pond, now dry, and the sluice can still be seen.

FRISTON

Donkey wheel, TQ548988. This stands outside Friston Place, on B2105 and once supplied Friston Place with water. The well-house is of brick and flint with a tiled roof and the wheel, 12ft (3·7m) diameter × 4ft 2in (1·27m) wide has a brake on the axle.

GLYNDE

Lime kiln, TQ458086. At the entrance to the chalk quarry opposite Glynde Station, N of A27. The quarry has been worked continuously since 1834. The old tunnel kiln, a square stone structure, may be seen on the right of the entrance, overlooking the old tramway cutting which goes under the road, and the exit of which can be seen at the end of the station platform. It originally extended down to a wharf on the R. Ouse. There used to be a double brick-built tunnel kiln in the hillside. The steam engine installed in 1824, which drove a crushing mill, was removed in 1940 and is preserved at LAUGHTON, Millwards Farm.

GROOMBRIDGE

Mile post, TQ530374. On W side of A264, the Tunbridge Wells–Maresfield Turnpike, established in 1766. Of local sandstone, much weathered, the only inscription being 'IV (i.e. 4 miles) to Tunbridge Wells'.

GUESTLING

Horse-gin, TQ846124. A late 19th-century outdoor horse-gin in the grounds of a private house near Hastings. It drives a 2-throw pump in a well alongside and originally supplied the house with water. It is in fair condition and the present owner is preserving it. There is also a small gas-holder for a private gas supply, probably acetylene.

HAILSHAM

Warehouse, TQ590101. Built in 1887, this 3-storey, brick-built decorated structure is still in use.

HAMSEY

Crossing-keeper's cottage, TQ409124. At a disused level crossing on a byroad leading to Hamsey Place Farm. A typical cottage of 1858 with grey tiles on the wall facing the track. It stands alongside the original track of the Lewes–Uckfield line, which was closed in 1868.

Hamsey Cut, TQ412123. A ½-mile (800m) straight cut across a loop of the river on the Upper Ouse Navigation crossed by an accommodation bridge on the road to Hamsey Place Farm. The outline of the chamber of Hamsey Lock can be seen just before the junction of the cut with the river at TQ407119.

HARTFIELD

Watermill, TQ481374. Bolebrook Mill, on the E side of B2026. A 19th-century brick and timber mill, it appears to be cared for and is used as a store. The overshot wheel, a wooden clasp-arm one, has collapsed, but the iron machinery and 2 pairs of stones remain.

HASTINGS

East Hill Lift, TQ823096. Until its electrification in 1974 this was one of the last water-balance cliff railways left in England. Of 5ft (1·5m) gauge, it is one of the steepest, having a length of 267ft (81·4m) at a gradient of 1:1.28 with 600 gallon (2728 litre) water tanks. Built in 1900–3 it runs in a cutting in the cliff face (Body, G. & Eastleigh, R.L., *Cliff Railways*, David & Charles, 1964, p 18).

Museum, TQ810095. The museum has an interesting display of the Wealden iron industry. This includes models, artifacts including a large number of cast-iron fire-backs, and a portion of the 16-century wooden waterwheel, excavated at Panningridge Furnace, which drove bellows for supplying air to the furnace. Also a section of the old iron railings round St Paul's Cathedral, which were cast at Lamberhurst, just over the county boundary in Kent.

Net shops, TQ827094. These tall, black wooden structures on the Stade or foreshore are used by the fishermen for storing their nets and other gear, not, as is often supposed, for drying the nets. They are of 2 or 3 storeys, weatherboarded with a pitched roof, access to the upper storeys being obtained by ladders clamped to the wall of the lower storeys inside. Each storey is owned or rented by a fisherman. The design is traditional and goes back to Elizabethan times; it is strictly maintained and preserved when repairing or rebuilding (*Plate 43*).

Old chimney, TQ816093. When the White Rock Baths were first established a steam engine was installed to pump sea water. In order to avoid disfiguring the promenade the chimney from the boiler house was carried under the road and the Palace Hotel (now Palace Chambers) to emerge behind the latter. The stump of this can still be seen on the seaward side of White Rock Gardens at the Prospect Place end; an octagonal brick structure, *c.*9ft (2·7m) high, and 6ft (1·8m) diameter.

Pier, TQ811091. Although built in 1872, the present appearance results from a major reconstruction of the sea front and buildings in the 1930s. It has been recommended for listing as a Grade II structure.

Railway viaduct, TQ818102. An attractive Victorian iron bridge with large fluted columns carries the Hastings–Ashford line over Queen's Road. It replaced a narrow brick arch of 1851 in the original embankment carrying the line across the valley.

West Hill Lift, TQ822095. Built in 1890 this cliff railway is unique in

43 Hastings: 'net shops' for storing nets and fishing gear

running for the whole of its length in a tunnel formed by extending a natural cave in the rock. It is 500ft (154m) long with a gradient of 1:3 and, although earlier driven by a small oil engine, it is now fully electrified. (Body, G. & Eastleigh, R.L., op. cit.).

HEATHFIELD

Natural gas works, TQ581206. A few yards from the lane leading NW from Sandy Cross on B2203 natural gas was found when drilling for water for the LB & SCR. Heathfield Station was lit by natural gas until the 1930s, but it was never used in the town. Started in 1896, a stand-pipe and derrick are now all that is left of the works.

HELLINGLEY

Watermill, TQ585125. On the R. Cuckmere, just W of a disused railway bridge over the road; ¼ mile (400m) NE of Hellingley Church. The 18th-century mill, of brick and timber construction, is privately owned. It has been preserved and is in very good condition, still containing most of the machinery. The sluice has been rebuilt by the present owner who hopes to restore the iron overshot wheel as well. There are also a well-preserved granary and bake-house. A mill has stood on this site since the 13th century.

HIGH HURSTWOOD

Farmbuildings, TQ482268. A complete set of Victorian farm buildings comprising barn, cowsheds, piggery, cart sheds, dairy and stores, all dating from the second half of the 19th century. At one end of the barn is a set of shafting originally used for driving chaff-cutter, root-cutter, thresher etc. from a small engine. Although neglected for the last 20 years, they are

in very fair condition and the present owner is progressively restoring them to a sound state for farming use again. **Watermill,** TQ493262. A small brick and timber building in fairly good condition with an iron overshot wheel, 18ft 6in (5·6m) diameter, and mainly wooden machinery. It dates from the late 18th or early 19th century.

HORAM

Cider press, TQ577173. An early 19th-century wooden cider press is preserved in the yard of the Merrydown Wine Co at Horam Manor.

HORSEBRIDGE

Toll house, TQ577115. A small brick-built cottage with a slate roof. The building is the original one but the front windows have apparently been replaced by larger ones. Situated on the N side of A221 it is now an antique shop. **Watermill,** TQ581113. On R. Cuckmere. A 3-storey whitewashed building with lucam, believed rebuilt in the late 19th or early 20th century after a fire. A 19th century iron breast-shot wheel, 16ft (4·9m) diameter, and sluice remain, the former in fair condition, the latter derelict, with the leat silted up. No other machinery is left. Now an electrically driven roller flour mill.

HOVE

Brighton & Hove Engineerium, TQ286066. This fine Victorian building, originally Goldstone Pumping Station (*Plate 44*), houses 2 beam engines, of 1866 and 1876, by Easton & Anderson, Erith, Kent, originally used for pumping water from 165ft (50m) deep wells to supply Brighton and Hove. The beams are 26ft 6in (8m) long and weigh 6 tonnes. There are 4 Lancashire boilers installed in 1934. Although the pumps have been disconnected, the No 2 engine (1876) has been restored to working order and is under steam at weekends; the No 1 engine (1866) will be restored to working order and put under steam in the near future. The original coal store has been converted into an exhibition hall and houses an exceptionally fine collection of model steam engines and mechanical devices, many of them made by famous Victorian engineers. The centre piece is the full-size Corliss horizontal steam engine that won 1st prize at the 1889 Paris Exhibition. The original workshop, with its overhead shafting driven by a small horizontal steam engine, has also been restored and is in active use for maintenance work and restoration of other engines.

Old railway, TQ280057–TQ261108. This very steep line branched off from the main line just W of Aldrington

Halt and climbed 400ft (122m) at an average gradient of 1 : 40 to its terminus c.200ft (61m) below the Devil's Dyke. Its route can still be traced through Hangleton and the Brighton & Hove Golf Course. The site of the upper terminus was at Devil's Dyke Farm.

ICKLESHAM

Hog Hill Windmill, TQ887160. On a side road S of A259 between Winchelsea and Pett. An early 18th-century post mill with round house. Originally at Pett, it was moved to its present site in 1785, and is reputed to date back to 1680. In fairly good condition externally with 4 sweeps, tail pole and fantail drive. Most of the internal machinery is present.

IDEN

Boundary stone, TQ940243. On the edge of the Royal Military Canal, between the canal and the road, where

44   Hove: Goldstone Pumping Station, now the Engineerium

it crosses the Kent Ditch, the Sussex–Kent boundary. A stone pillar with hemispherical top, it was put up when the canal was cut and bears the date 1806 and the county names (*Plate 45*). **Lock,** TQ936244. On the Royal Military Canal at its junction with the R. Rother. Much of the masonry is original and in 1958 when renewals were made at the upper end, the lower halves of two of the original lock gates were found beneath an old earth dam. The lock cottage is contemporary with the lock, early 19th century. The lower lock gates still remain, but the upper gates are missing and a rotary sluice above the locks blocks the navigation. The gates were designed to work in both directions; presumably the R. Rother was tidal up to here when the canal was cut.

ISFIELD

Railway station, TQ452121. On the Lewes–Uckfield line. Track lifted but crossing gates remain. Main buildings derelict and subject to vandalism. Signal box in fair condition with frame and levers intact. Coal siding with bins behind access road.
Watermill, TQ449181. A 100-year-old building with water turbine driving stones, now used for animal feed only.

LAUGHTON

Old engines, TQ516124. At Millwards Farm on the S side of A273 *c.*1 mile (1·6km) E of village. Mr Baker has completely restored the 40HP steam engine removed from Glynde Chalk Pit. There is also a Ruston hot-bulb engine in full working order. In addition he has a 12-cylinder Rolls-Royce Griffon aero-engine, for contra-rotating props, and two 18-cylinder Wright Cyclone radial aero-engines, which he hopes to restore. Open to the public.

45 Iden: Kent/Sussex boundary stone on the Royal Military Canal

Toll house, TQ483128. Built in 1766 for the Broyle Park Gate–Battle Turnpike, it is of brick with additions at the rear, and lies on the S side of A273. Originally of only 2 rooms (1 up and 1 down). The toll-keeper's viewing window on the 1st floor is still discernible though now blocked.

LEWES

Anne of Cleves House Museum, TQ412097. Owned by the Sussex Archaeological Society, it houses, among other exhibits, a very fine display of artifacts relating to the Wealden iron industry. As well as a wide range of cast-iron fire-backs there is a portion of the waterwheel excavated at the 16th-century Chingley Forge which drove the trip hammer, and also a boring-bar for cast-iron cannon, probably dating from the early 17th century and possibly unique.

Ashcombe toll house, TQ389093. A small circular, single-storey brick building with a domed roof (*Plate 46*). It was never lived in and was one of a pair dating from c.1810. At present isolated beside the road from Kingston where this joins A27. It is being preserved during the construction of the Lewes southern bypass and will be left standing beside the A27.

Beard's brewery, TQ414102. The 18th-century malthouse and brewery buildings still remain though brewing ceased a few years ago and it is now a bottling works. The boilerhouse and chimney for the 19th-century steam engine can be seen from the lane behind. The engine is to be transferred to Harveys Brewery and preserved there. The old brewing machinery still remains.

Road bridge, TQ419102. Across the R. Ouse, it joins the High Streets of Lewes and Cliffe. Built in 1727, of brick and stone c.10ft (3m) wide, it was designed by Nicholas Dubois, the architect of Stanmer House, near Brighton. The overhanging pavement on the N side was added in 1808 and a replica was built against the S face in 1931–3 to widen the roadway.

Harvey's Brewery, TQ419103. On the E bank of the R. Ouse, just N of Cliffe Bridge. At least 200 years of continuous brewing history on the site though the present buildings and tower were put up in 1880 (*Plate 47*). A 19th-century horizontal steam engine, which originally drove the machinery, is still preserved, and another engine transferred from Beard's Brewery will also be preserved here.

Old candle factory, TQ416102. This 3-storey 18th-century brick building fronting on Market Lane was used as a candle factory by Broad's from the 1820s to the end of the 19th century. The name James Broad appears on the house alongside, and 2 boxes of candles from the last dip and the board giving conditions of employment are preserved in the museum at Anne of Cleves House. The bracket for the hand hoist remains over the loading door on the first floor and some of the cast-iron windows are probably original. The last survivor of the many factory buildings that once thrived in Lewes, there is some hope that it may be preserved and used for craft workshops and studios.

Southdown Brewery, TQ421104. On the W side of A26 just beyond its junction with A27. An early 19th-century building in the classical style at the end of a street of old brick cottages. No brewing equipment remains.

Malling toll house, TQ426122. On A26, the Lewes–Uckfield road, which was turnpiked in 1752. A single-storey rectangular building c.37ft (11·31m) × 13ft (4m), with 7ft (2·1m)

46   Lewes: Ashcombe toll house

walls and a slate roof. There was a projecting porch, since enlarged.

Milestone, TQ411100. A late 18th-century stone tablet in the face of a 15th-century timber-framed building which is now a bookshop. The inscription reads '50 MILES/FROM THE STANDARD/IN CORNHILL/49 TO WESTMINSTER BRIDGE/8 MILES TO BRIGHTHELM-STONE'. Being within the town boundary it was not erected by a turnpike trust but by the borough of Lewes.

Old station, TQ419101. The site of the 1846 station can be seen on the E side of Friars' Walk. The 1868 line crossed Cliffe High Street at TQ418102, where the abutments can still be seen on either side. The embankment can be traced for 100yd (91m) or more to N and S of this point.

Warehouses, TQ419101. S of Cliffe High Street, on the W bank of the R. Ouse, there are two granaries, which were substantially rebuilt after a fire in 1912, at which date barges still worked up to Lewes. Strickland's is slate hung (*Plate 48*) with a lucam on the landward side, and Stevenson's is of red brick and somewhat altered in recent years.

MAGHAM DOWN

Amberstone toll house, TQ599113. On the S side of A271. Except for a small extension to the rear it is almost as originally built, though the front door has been bricked up. The small side window, for ease of observation by the toll-keeper, can be seen. It was built in 1776 for the Battle–Broyle Park Gate turnpike.

MARESFIELD

Watermill, TQ457264. Boring Wheel

47 Lewes: Harvey's Brewery

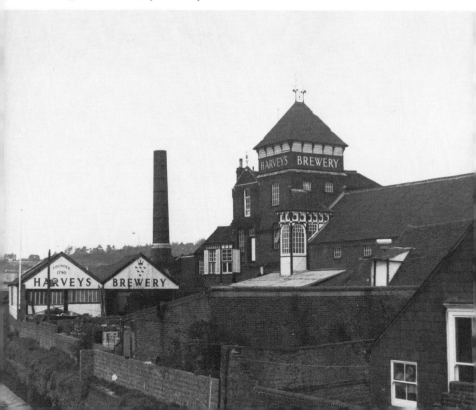

48   Lewes: granary on bank of R. Ouse

Mill. An 18th/19th-century brick and timber building on the site of a former iron works. In fair condition and now used as a store and workshop. The waterwheel has gone but the wooden shaft and hubs remain. The wooden vertical shaft and iron machinery are still there with 1 pair of stones.

MAYFIELD

Watermill, TQ591249. Moat Mill. On R. Rother, $\frac{1}{4}$ mile (400m) E of the Heathfield–Mayfield road, and $1\frac{1}{4}$ miles (2km) SSE of Mayfield. A small 18th-century brick and timber building with iron overshot wheel and the original wooden machinery. Now converted into part of a dwelling house, but the waterwheel and machinery have been retained. The water-supply channel is now dry.

MOUNTFIELD

Gypsum mine, TQ720195. Dating from c.1870 the mine is still active, processing gypsum for plaster and plasterboard, and shale for roadstone. There is a cable railway for $3\frac{1}{4}$ miles (5·6km) to a second mine near Brightling (TQ677217).

NEWHAVEN

Tide mills, TQ459001. At Bishopstone, $\frac{1}{2}$ mile (800m) E of the mouth of the R. Ouse at Newhaven. An access road leaves A259 at TQ463004 and crosses the railway to the site of the mills. Begun in 1762 and much extended c.1800 to contain 15 pairs of stones, they were closed in the 1890s. The walls and foundations of cottages and stores remain and 3 wheel tunnels in the dam, which contained undershot wheels c.15ft (4·6m) diameter. The main reservoir is to the E and another one was later added to the W. Frag-ments of the sluice gates in the tunnels still remain.

Harbour works, the Western breakwater, 1000yd (914m) long, TQ447999–452993, was built in concrete in 1879–84. It allows a sufficient depth of water at all states of the tide. There is an old lighthouse at the seaward end of it. On the E bank of the river some of the old railway and marine workshops, built in 1878, also survive.

NEWICK

Oast house, TQ437194. On Vuggles Farm, just E of the minor road from Barcombe Cross to Newick. The oast house and barn are complete and in fairly good condition though the normal conical roof of the oast has been replaced by a pitched tiled roof. The oast is complete and unaltered inside and includes the hearth holes and drying floor.

Sharpsbridge lock, TQ443200. c.500yd (447m) below the road bridge on W side of R. Ouse, opposite the entrance to Shortbridge branch. Lock cut now silted up. A few masonry remains of the lock are left, much eroded and overgrown.

Village pump, TQ419213. Situated on the village green, this was put up by the residents to commemorate the Diamond Jubilee of 1897.

NINFIELD

Barn and oast, TQ703124. An early 19th-century brick construction, these farm buildings are in good condition and are the subject of a preservation order.

Iron stocks, TQ707124. Cast-iron and wrought-iron stocks and whipping post which were made locally, at Ashburnham or possibly Lamberhurst.

NORTHIAM

Builder's workshop, TQ848246. The Perigoe Workshop Museum stands on the W side of A28 just N of a car park on the E side. It is an 18th-century timber structure, having belonged to a Will Perigoe in 1785, and is now preserved by the widow of the last Perigoe to use it. There is a very complete set of old carpenter's tools, many of them handmade, with possibly the finest collection of moulding planes in the country. There is also a paint shop and plumber's and pipe fitter's shop and a collection of miscellaneous builders' tools and equipment. Open Wednesdays or by appointment.

Village pump, TQ830245. This is an open wooden structure with a brick base and tiled roof. It stands, on the village green just off A28. The pump is of cast iron and a plaque gives its date as 1907.

NUTLEY

Windmill, TQ451291. c.¼ mile (400m). N of Marlpits c.1 mile (1·6km) from Nutley on the Crowborough road. A late 17th-century post mill with open trestle. The oldest post mill in Sussex and the only example of this primitive type (*Plate 49*). Tailpole but no fantail. Two pairs of stones. Fully restored to working order in 1973 by the Uckfield & District Preservation Society, it grinds corn regularly. New spring sails were fitted in 1973. Open last Sunday of each month, June to September, or by appointment.

OFFHAM

Lime kilns, TQ400116. In the quarries behind the Chalk Pit Inn, on the W side of A275, c.⅓ mile (540m) S of the village. Four kilns are visible though much overgrown, 3 round ones and 1 tall square one. A tramway runs from the innyard in 2 brick-arched tunnels under the road and then down a very steep scarp to a wharf on a cut from the R. Ouse (TQ402116). First used in 1809 and out of use by 1890, it is the oldest railway in Sussex.

Toll house, TQ400122. A cottage at the S end of the village street, on the W side is an enlarged toll house. The original building was probably a small brick rectangular structure with a projecting porch. The road was turnpiked in 1752.

PATCHAM

Windmill, TQ291087. S of A2038, c.½ mile (800m) from its junction with A23. A brick tower mill built in 1885 and probably the last working mill to be constructed in Sussex. Now a dwelling house but most of the iron machinery has been retained. New sweeps were fitted in 1972 and the fantail repaired.

PIDDINGHOE

Kiln, TQ433032. At the N end of Piddinghoe village on the Newhaven–Lewes road, in the grounds of Kiln Cottage. The last conical brick-built kiln in Sussex, and the only survivor of its type in the county, its cone can be easily seen from the road. Though rather covered with vegetation it is preserved by the owner and is in tolerably good condition seeing that it was built in 1805. It has been used for pottery, tiles and bricks and was last operated in 1912. There were originally 6 kilns on the site, 4 at the N end for tiles and 2 at the S end for whiting.

PLAYDEN

Folk museum, TQ922214. A small private museum with an interesting

49 Nutley: the oldest post mill in Sussex

display of agricultural and farmhouse implements has been established by Mrs Townsend at Cherries, Playden, Rye. Open to the public.

Scots Float Lock, TQ933227. A tidal lock on the canalized section of the R. Rother. The lock gates and the sluices are arranged to work in both directions as the river is tidal below the lock. The lower and middle gates are original but the upper ones are modern. On the upstream side of the road bridge is a plaque with inscription: 'ERECTED A.D. 1844/WILLIAM CUBITT ESQRE / ENGINEER / JAMES ELLIOTT / DESIGNER & BUILDER'.

PLUMPTON

Watermill, TQ363147. Upper Mill. A small 19th-century brick and timber building with a gambrel roof, iron overshot wheel, iron machinery and 2 pairs of stones. In remarkably good condition it is being restored to working order by its owner.

Watermill, TQ363150. Plumpton Mill. A 19th-century brick and timber building, re-roofed c.1962. The iron overshot wheel and iron machinery are used to drive an electric generator, the drive being taken from a bevel ring below the great spur wheel though it was originally by belt drive from the auxiliary shaft. There are no stones left.

POLEGATE

Cannon, TQ597065. On NE side of B2104. A cast-iron cannon of George III's reign with the GR monogram. The cannon is rifled and the date is too late for it to have come from a Sussex gun foundry. It may possibly be removed to some better place for preservation. Property of the East Sussex CC. It has now been decided to remove the cannon to Westham where it will be mounted on the grass triangle outside the Western entrance of Pevensey Castle at TQ643046.

Windmill, TQ581041. In the centre of the village, just W of A22. A fine brick-built tower mill, partly tile-hung, dating from 1817. Restored in 1967 by the Eastbourne & District Preservation Society, it is in full working order, and has a milling museum attached (*Plate 50*). Open to the public every Sunday from May to October, or by appointment. One of the sweeps broke recently and it is hoped to replace it in the near future.

PRESTON

Horse-gin, TQ305065. In Preston Park, Brighton. Housed in a flint-built well-house adjoining the churchyard, mid 19th century. It supplied water to the manor house. Preserved by Brighton Corporation but not open to the public.

Malthouse, TQ302064. In South Road, Brighton. Built by a small publican who made his own malt and beer. Probably late 18th century. It has a single floor 30ft (9m) long and the kiln is only 10ft (3m) high. The building, of flint with brick quoins, is now used as a store.

PUNNETS TOWN

Windmill, TQ627208. On the N side of B2096. A 19th-century smock mill on a brick base. Machinery intact with 2 pairs of stones and 4 common sails. Originally at Biddenden, Kent, it was moved to its present site in 1856. Known as Cherry Clack Mill or Blackdown Mill. The iron wind shaft came from Stapelcross smock mill.

RINGMER

Broyle Side toll house, TQ463132.

50 Polegate: tower mill

On A205 which was turnpiked in 1768. A very small black, boarded cottage, with a crooked chimney. Probably dates from the 18th century.

Village pump, TQ449126. At the N corner of the village green on the N side of A265. The well and pump, with an open wooden framework and tiled roof, were constructed and presented to Ringmer Parish in 1883.

ROBERTSBRIDGE

Coldharbour toll house, TQ719235. On the S side of the Robertsbridge–Brightling road. The original building was a 2-roomed brick cottage, and an extra floor and more rooms at the back have been added. Built in 1813 for the Beech Down–Hoods Corner turnpike.

Old wooden crane, TQ734235. In a small 19th-century warehouse in the station yard, now leased to the post office, is an interesting hand-operated wooden crane. The operation of this is by an endless rope over a large diameter pulley at the head of the upright member; a small diameter drum on the pulley shaft then winds in the chain over the pulley at the end of the jib, thus giving a useful reduction in effort without the need to wind in many yards of rope (*Plate 51*).

Watermill, TQ737241. Garner-Hodson's Mill, on the W side of A23. A large 19th-century brick-built flour mill, now used only for animal feeds. A disused iron overshot wheel *c*.9ft (2·7m) diameter remains in a culvert under the building. The bypass sluice also still exists.

ROTHERFIELD

Windmill, TQ570283. Argos Hill Mill stands on the S side of B2101, between Rotherfield and Mayfield, just W of its junction with A267. A very fine late 18th-century post mill with round-

house and fantail at the end of the tail-pole. All machinery is present and there is an interesting collection of milling artifacts in the roundhouse. The mill has been fully restored and is preserved by the Crowborough DC. Open by appointment.

Iron grave slab, TQ556297. A single cast-iron slab in the floor of the church with no date or inscription, only the double cross of Lorraine. Probably not as old as this might suggest (see BURWASH, TQ677247).

ROTTINGDEAN

Windmill, TQ366025. On the hill above the coast road. A smock mill on a brick base of the late 18th century, it was moved to its present site in 1802. It ground flour for Challoner's Farm until the 1880s. Maintained by the Rottingdean Preservation Society, although outwardly complete and of good appearance, it has been strengthened inside with steel girders that have rendered the machinery mostly inacessible. The outline of this mill has been used for the motif of Heinemann's, the publishers.

RYE

Brede Lock, TQ920199. An early 19th-century lock on the R. Brede at its junction with the R. Tillingham. The lock gates have recently been rebuilt and are arranged to work in both directions as the R. Tillingham is tidal at this point. A new road bridge now crosses the middle of the lock chamber.

Cistern, TQ922203. Behind the church in a corner of the churchyard. Built in 1735 it is one of the most remarkable examples of architectural brickwork in Sussex, if not in England. Only the upper half can be seen from the road as the cistern itself is largely below ground level. It is built on an oval plan

51 Robertsbridge: wooden crane in station yard

with a domed roof to meet the central oval tower. There are no straight walls, all being of varying radius, and the domed inner and outer roofs of the cistern have varying radii in two directions. Altogether a real masterpiece of bricklaying. A hand pump in front is dated to 1826 (*SIH* No 7 Spring 1976 p 24).

Horse-gin, TQ901192. On S side of B2089 at Watland's Farm. Octagonal timber-built, it is erected against the side of a barn and originally drove various machines in the barn. No machinery remains.

Old water works, TQ921205. Now converted to a public lavatory the building bears the date 1869 on the S end. When excavating for the conversion parts of the old wooden pump mechanism were found, including a lantern pinion *c.*3ft (91cm) in diameter.

Railway goods shed, TQ919205. Just SW of the station. The goods shed, now a private transport garage, contains an interesting old hand-operated wooden crane.

Railway station, TQ918205. Built in 1851 to the designs of William Tress who was responsible for most of the SER stations in Sussex. Brick with stone quoins and facings it is in the Italianate style with a 3-arched portico. There is a small crossing-keeper's cottage to the E.

Toll house, TQ914205. On B2089 near the bridge over the R. Tillingham. A 2-roomed brick cottage with tiled roof, now used as a workshop.

Warehouse, TQ918204. At the level crossing on Ferry Road (B2080) on the S side of the road. A large 3-storey 19th century building marked 'Foremans Corn, Hop and Seed Stores' now a pottery. On the N side of the road is an attractive small wooden cabin for the crossing-keeper.

Warehouses, TQ928202. A fine group of warehouses on the Strand beside the river (*Plate 52*). The oldest, known as the 'Grist Mill', was built *c.*1736 from stone brought over as ballast from France. It is in good condition and is being preserved. The others, timber-framed and boarded on a brick base, are in poor condition but it is hoped they may be preserved. One of them is unusual in having a rounded corner, facing the river.

Windmill, TQ916203. Just off A259 at the entrance to Rye from the S. A smock mill on brick base. Only the shell of the building remains, put up to replace a mill burnt down in 1929. No machinery is left, and the cap and sweeps cannot turn.

RYE HARBOUR

Old pier, TQ949173. Now the Port of Rye. The E pier dates from 1845.

ST LEONARD'S

Toll house, TQ797093. North Lodge bridges Maze Hill, the approach road to Burton's St Leonard's from the N. Built in 1830, the last toll was taken in 1837 when the present London Road from Silverhill to the sea-front was made. The house is attractively battlemented and is now a private dwelling.

Ventilating shaft, TQ796092. A 19th-century oval brick-built shaft ventilates the railway tunnel between Warrior Square and West St Leonard's and emerges surprisingly on an island in the middle of Pevensey Road.

SALEHURST

Iron grave slabs, TQ749248. In the floor at the base of the tower are 4 cast-iron slabs marking the burials of Mary, William, Eleanor and Sylveste Peckham. Dates 1672 to 1713. One of these, Mary, was an infant burial. All in good condition.

SCAYNES HILL

Freshfield Lock, TQ385244. The chamber of this lock, on the Upper Ouse Navigation, can be seen on the upstream side of the road bridge, opposite the Sloop Inn, which was in existence when the navigation was fully opened in 1812.

SEDLESCOMBE

Iron grave slab, TQ777188. In floor at W end of N aisle. It marks the burial of William, Elizabeth and Sarah Bisshop, dates 1629 to 1669. In good condition.

Pump and well house, TQ782179. Built in 1900 this stands in the middle of the village green and rather resembles a market cross. Until a few years ago it was the main village water supply.

Toll house, TQ776204. On the W side of A229. Brick and timber-framed with weatherboarding. Built in 1836 for the Hastings–Sedlescombe–Cripps Corner Turnpike Trust.

SHEFFIELD PARK

Bacon Wish Lock, TQ398240. On the Upper Ouse Navigation, it may be reached by walking along the river bank from Sheffield Bridge towards Freshfield Bridge. The lock walls are well preserved and there is an accommodation bridge. The lock was first opened to traffic c.1799.

Mile post, TQ411246. Outside the main entrance to Sheffield Park on a bank on the W side of A275 stands a tall sandstone shaft with a domed cap, c.9ft 3in (2·8m) high, with the distances to East Grinstead, Lewes, Brighthelmstone and Westminster Bridge carved on the sides of the cap. It is not a turnpike trust's milestone and was probably erected by the 1st Earl of Sheffield in 1780.

52   Rye: stone warehouse known as the 'Grist Mill'

Railway station, TQ403237. The southern terminus and headquarters of the Bluebell Railway. The Bluebell line originally extended from East Grinstead to Lewes, being opened in 1882 and closed in 1955. The Bluebell Railway from Sheffield Park Station to Horsted Keynes (W Sussex) was opened in 1964, the track having been preserved here. Both stations have been very well restored and a fine collection of vintage steam locomotives and rolling stock operate a public service. It is hoped it may be possible to extend the track from Horsted Keynes to East Grinstead.

SHORTGATE

Brickworks, TQ478142. On NW side of A265. Bricks were still being made by hand a few years ago by an unusual method. The stack of bricks acted as its own kiln, fuel being placed between the layers of bricks as the stack was built. There was also a pug mill driven by an oil engine.

SOUTHERHAM

Lime kilns, TQ426095. The Eastwood Cement Works on A27 S of Lewes. It is fairly modern, but one building contains an electric motor removed from a German submarine in 1918.

STANMER

Donkey wheel, TQ336096. A 13ft-(4m)-diameter wheel in a small flint house in the corner of the churchyard, which drew water from a 252ft- (77m)-deep well. It may date from the 16th century and was operated by a donkey until 1870, and then by man-power until 1900. Although the door of the building is kept locked the wheel may be seen through a glass panel in the door, illuminated by electric light

controlled by a time switch. The wheelhouse was rebuilt in 1838.

Horse-gin, TQ336095. Housed in an open-sided timber-framed well house, the wheel was equipped for two horses and drew from a well, now covered over, to supply Stanmer House. It dates from 1724–7 though the well is older. There is an old tyring platform displayed beside the horse-gin and a small agricultural museum behind Stanmer House.

STONE CROSS

Windmill, TQ624043. Just S of A27 in the middle of the village. A late 19th-century tower mill with ogee cap on a cast-iron frame. All machinery is present and the fantail was restored a few years ago; 2 sweeps remain and the owner hopes to supply 2 more and restore the mill to working order in the near future.

STONEGATE

Railway station, TQ658272. A simple building in the Italianate style, in stucco. Built in 1851 it is one of William Tresse's designs for the SER. A 2-storey station master's house and single-storey station building whose roof extends over the platform; a device also used at Robertsbridge.

TICEHURST

Toll house, TQ685304. On the N side of A266. A 2-roomed weatherboarded cottage with tiled roof and extra rooms added at the E end. Built for the Flimwell–Hastings Trust in 1762.

UCKFIELD

Watermill, TQ452213. Shortbridge Mill. A 19th-century brick and timber building, gutted internally and now used as a store. The iron pitch-back wheel, 9ft (2·7m) diameter, and elaborate cast-iron penstock dating from c.1870 still remain.

Watermill, TQ483217. Hempstead Mill. A 19th-century brick and timber building in fairly good condition, used as a garage and store for the mill house. The iron breast-shot wheel drove an electric generator for heating the mill house. Some machinery remains.

UPPER DICKER

Watermill (Michelham Priory), TQ557093. The 18th-century building is timber-framed and boarded. A water-wheel and complete internal machinery were installed 1974–6 by the Sussex Archaeological Society, who own Michelham Priory. The mill is supplied with water from the moat which is fed from the R. Cuckmere.

Wheelwright's shop etc, TQ558093. At Michelham Priory a wheelwright's and blacksmith's shop has been reconstructed and there are several farm waggons and carts displayed.

WADHURST

Iron grave slabs, TQ641319. This church contains 30 cast-iron slabs in the floor of the chancel, nave and aisles. Nearly all of them mark the burials of Barhams, possibly ancestors of the author of the *Ingoldsby Legends*. Dates from 1617 to 1771. The earliest one has the date but no inscription. The others vary in the degree of legibility of the inscription.

Toll house, TQ644313. On the S side of A266. A 2-roomed whitewashed, brick cottage with slate roof. The window at the E end has been enlarged and the W end extended to form a small cobbler's shop. The observation window in the E wall is still discernible, though bricked up.

WEST BLATCHINGTON

Windmill, TQ278068. Just S of A2038. A 6-floored hexagonal smock mill on top of a square tower forming part of a barn. The mill was built c.1724 and worked until 1900. The main drive remains intact but there is no provision for working the stones. The mill is unusual, in being hexagonal, in having a cross for the sweeps instead of the more usual poll end, and in having an additional power take-off for driving farm machinery in the barn. It also has a particularly fine cast-iron curb supporting the cap. It was the subject of a painting by Constable. The Mill belongs to the Borough of Hove DC and it is hoped to restore the mill and establish a small museum there.

WESTFIELD

Hydraulic ram, TQ825136. In a domed underground brick chamber c.8ft (2·4m) diameter × 10ft (3m) high. The ram drew from a pond behind a brick dam and delivered water to a tank in New Coghurst Farm.

Water storage tank, TQ828132. Above the W bank of the stream in the grounds of Coghurst Hall, now a residential caravan site. The brick-built tank, c.20ft (6m) in diameter by 8ft (2·4m) deep, with a domed roof, and holding about 5,000 gallons (22,750 litres) was fed by a spring yielding only c.250 gallons (1,150 litres) per hour and supplied the hall.

WILMINGTON

Museum, TQ544042. The agricultural museum at Wilmington Priory houses a very fine collection of agricultural tools and implements, amongst which is an unusual portable horse-gin found on a farm near Ringmer. The drive was taken off by two extension shafts with universal joints to operate various machines about the farm.

WINCHELSEA

Well and well house, TQ906175. In Castle Street on the N side of the town. A small stone building over the well head and open on 3 sides contains the headgear and cast-iron outlet spout. A shaft with double handles drove a 2-throw pump through gearing. It dates from 1831 and supplied water to the town until a few years ago.

Windmill, TQ902176. St Leonard's Mill. Just W of the N end of the town. A post mill with round house, dating from c.1760. The exterior has been restored but there are no sweeps. The machinery is mainly intact, though the windshaft is missing. The body has had to be underpinned as the crowntree is cracked. The mill may be threatened by a proposed bypass N of the town.

WINDMILL HILL

Windmill, TQ647122. On a small hill just to the N of A271 in the middle of the village. A tall 3-storey post mill on top of a tall 2-storey roundhouse. In rather poor condition, with the body covered with sheet iron except on the tail, where the weatherboarding is rotten and the door permanently open.

Machinery and stones intact but no sweeps. Late 18th century. It has a unique governor driven off the windshaft. Efforts are being made to restore the mill.

WITHYHAM

Water pump, TQ499352. On the Buckhurst Park Estate, a small 3-throw pump driven by an overshot wheel c.10ft (3m) diameter supplied water to the gardens and fountains of the house. Though long out of use it is in not too bad condition and it is proposed to restore it to working order again.

WYCH CROSS

Pippingford Furnace, TQ450316. Two separate furnaces have been excavated, dating from the early 18th century. A complete gun-casting pit has also been excavated. The site is being taken into guardianship by the Department of the Environment.

Milestone, TQ419317. A sandstone slab set in a brick frame, originally in the wall of the toll house demolished in 1965. It is inscribed 'To Maresfield 6 Miles/from Maresfield to Uckfield 1 Mile half/from Uckfield to Lewes 7 Miles half/and this is the Toll Road to Lewes'. It may well date from 1752 when the Malling Street to Wych Cross Turnpike Trust was founded.

West Sussex

The Arun Navigation and the Wey & Arun Canal provide an extensive and interesting field for the industrial archaeologist (PLATE 53). In 1787 the Arun Navigation was opened as far as Newbridge, though the Hardham Tunnel cutting off the long loop through Pulborough was not completed until 1790. The Wey & Arun Canal starts at Newbridge and crosses over into Surrey near Loxwood (for further details see under SURREY). Opened in 1816 it reached its peak traffic in 1839 and was closed in 1871; it rises 64ft (19·5m) in 7 miles (11·3km) to the county boundary, through 8 locks, 75ft (22·8m) × 13ft (4m), the summit level being about 1 mile (1·6km) over the border in Surrey. Although parts of it are still in water round Billingshurst and further N most is dry and derelict but being steadily restored by the efforts of the Wey & Arun Canal Trust. The Rother Navigation, which joins the Arun near Pulborough, was opened in 1794 but was abandoned by 1888. A very full account of the history of these navigations and the competition from the railways is given in P.A.L. Vine's *London's Lost Route to the Sea*, which also gives details of other waterways in W Sussex and Surrey.

Several of the old abandoned railway lines can be walked and the old stations inspected. Where these have been converted into private houses they are preserved, but the disused ones, whether on abandoned lines or on those still in use, tend to disappear as a result of development, or demolition by British Rail; many have vanished completely.

ALDINGBOURNE

Watermill, SU925049. A 19th-century mill and mill house under the same roof. The bin floor of the mill has been incorporated into the mill house to form bedrooms, but the mill is otherwise intact and in good condition. Iron overshot wheel and iron machinery with a tee-shaped hursting and 3 pairs of stones.

AMBERLEY

Industrial museum, TQ028118. An open-air museum and educational centre, the Chalk Pits Museum, Amberley, is being established by the Trustees of the Southern Industrial History Centre in the old chalk pits behind Amberley Station. Much material for this is already in store and, among other exhibits, there will be sections dealing with brick-making, iron-founding and lime works. There is a very fine range of disused lime kilns on the site which will be restored, and the contents of a 19th-century jobbing iron foundry from Hurst Green in E Sussex, probably the last to work in the area, were dismantled and are now in store, together with many other items illustrating the industrial history of the south of England. It is hoped to be able to open the museum to the public in 1979.

ANSTY

Watermill, TQ287212. There are a

Wey and Arun Canal

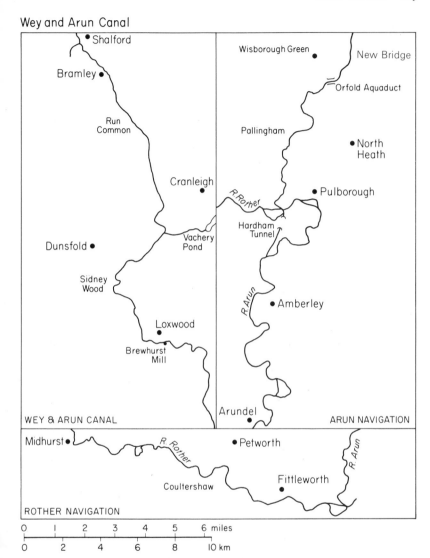

53 Map showing Wey & Arun Canal and Arun & Rother Navigations

few remains of this 19th-century small brick and timber mill, though it is now completely derelict. The waterwheel has gone but the iron shaft and some internal machinery survive.

ARUNDEL

Horse-gin, TQ012066. The brick and flint roundhouse with a slate roof can be seen just inside the premises of James Penfold Ltd on the road to Ford. It was originally used for crushing linseed for an oil-cake mill.

Castle ice-house, TQ015075. A square chamber of late construction still remains at the castle.

Warehouses, TQ019070. S along the river. Until the opening of the Wey & Arun Canal in 1816, the bulk of the shipping entering the R Arun berthed at Arundel and warehouses and granaries still existing on the W bank S of the bridge are a testimony to the importance of the port. There is a particularly fine warehouse, in flint and yellow brick with a slate roof, at the bottom of Arun Street and a double brick and timber one, now an antique market, in River Road.

Water-pumping station, TQ018077. There is an interesting little building of ecclesiastical appearance on the Arundel Castle Estate which originally pumped water up to a reservoir on the hill above to supply the town. Although apparently of flint the walls are actually of brick with a thin flint facing. The building contains a water turbine fed from the adjacent Swanbourne Lake under a head of c.10ft (3m) and discharging into the tidal R. Arun; it drives 2 triple-throw pumps through reduction gearing. Though the building has been roofless for more than 10 years the machinery is still in moderately good condition. Water was pumped from a well and underground streams to the reservoir on the hill

which had the date 1844 marked on it. The future of this installation is still uncertain.

Windmill, TQ013063. On the E bank of the Arun, a black tower mill with a brown cap but no sweeps. It dates from 1840 and is now part of a dwelling house.

BALCOMBE

Viaduct, TQ323278. This fine viaduct built 1839–41, carries the London–Brighton line over the Ouse Valley. It is 1475ft (450m) long and 96ft (29·3m) above the river, with 37 semicircular arches (*Plate 54*). Built by John Raistrick of Stourbridge, it has 4 attractive stone pavilions at each end. Materials for the construction were brought by the Ouse Navigation whose terminus, at Upper Rylands Bridge, was adjacent.

Water-pumping station, TQ330320. In the valley of Ardingley Brook. Top of building may be seen from entrance of private drive at Little Strudgate Farm. Derelict remains of an early 20th-century pumping station containing the remains of two 3-throw pumps which may have supplied Wakehurst Place. There are plinths for engines or motor bed-plates beside the pumps with reduction gears still existing showing that the drive was either from oil or gas engines or electric motors. There are settling tanks behind the building and the remains of 2 hydraulic rams in a shed on the bank of the stream. The date 1901 is carved on the cottages at the entrance to the private road, which are probably contemporary with the pumping station.

BALLS CROSS

Watermill, SU981281. Wassell Mill stands on a tributary of the R. Arun c.½ mile (800m) E of Ebernoe House. A brick and timber building, now a dwelling house; the iron overshot wheel can be seen from the road.

BARLAVINGTON

Watermill, TQ979180. Burton Mill, built in 1781, is a large 4-storey stone building which originally had 2 water-wheels on the E and W sides, each driving at least 2 pairs of stones. Both wheels have been replaced by turbines; the older one on the E side has several parts missing and is in poor condition, but the one on the W side, dating from 1929, appears to be still in usable condition. It is an inward flow reaction turbine of Francis type, and its name-plate is marked 'William Dell'. There is no milling machinery and the W turbine was arranged to drive a saw bench on the ground floor through an an extensive system of line shafting and belt drives. The bin floor at the top of the building remains sub-stantially intact with sack-hoist, screw-feed for grain and belt-drive from the floor below. There is a possibility that the mill may be restored. The pond, now an extensive lake, is in good condition and there is a nature reserve on the E side of the lake.

BARNHAM

Windmill, SU968038. A black tower mill of 1790. Only the tower remains, in fairly good condition, inside the works of John Baker (miller & corn merchant). The windshaft and brake wheel remains, though there are no sweeps, and the fan-tail gallery has been removed. The machinery is modern.

BIRDHAM

Saltern's Lock, SU826012. The sole remaining working lock on the Ports-mouth & Arundel Canal, 8ft (2·4m)

54 Balcombe: railway viaduct on London–Brighton line

deep to take seagoing vessels; at the exit of the canal into tidal waters, but only used by pleasure craft now. There is a swing bridge a little way E of the lock. The site of the old tide-mill is now occupied by a yacht club.

BOGNOR REGIS

Old aircraft factory, SU979000. The factory was built c.1914 for White & Thompson Ltd (later Norman Thompson Co Ltd) and was closed in 1919 after being acquired by Handley Page Ltd. It is now a holiday camp.

Ice-house, SZ936995. This is situated beside the public library in London Road and originally served the Hotham Estate. It can be seen from outside the library (*Plate 55*). It dates from c.1797 and has been restored and is maintained by the local authority. The walls are of random brick and flint construction with brick corners and a brick

dome c.10ft (3m) in diameter.

Pier, SZ934987. This pleasure pier was built in 1865 at a cost of c.£5000, and is c.1000ft (305m) long.

BROADBRIDGE

Watermill, SU812063. Ratham Mill, a 19th-century brick building now used as a store with a modern mill built alongside. The iron overshot wheel, iron gears and wooden vertical shaft remain; also a turbine which drove a generator for supplying electricity.

BUCKS GREEN

Railway bridge, TQ094327. The only surviving river crossing on the old LB & SCR line from Horsham to Guildford, it carried the line over the R. Arun, c.350yd (320m) S of A281. Built in 1865 it was closed in 1965. The original bridge was a single brick arch

55   Bognor Regis: Ice-house

but was never used as the approach embankments were subject to slipping. They were reinforced and raised and a cast-iron girder built in c.10ft (3m) above the top of the arch (*Plate 56*). It may be reached by walking along the old railway track from the point where it crossed A281.

Watermill, TQ072308. Gibbons Mill on the R. Arun, c.1½ miles (2·4km) S of Bucks Green, is a wooden corn mill on stone foundations, at least 300 years old, with a brick extension to the N added c.1860. The undershot water wheel was replaced, c.1900 by a vertical shaft turbine driving a dynamo, and also a water pump, by belting. In 1930 the original turbine was replaced by an Armfield turbine of 16hp (11·9w) working under a 9ft 6in (2·9m) head, and in 1946 the dynamo and switchboard were replaced. The original switchboard and a watt-hour meter of c.1900 are preserved. The mill cottage

and mill are now a private residence.

BURGESS HILL

Bakehouse, TQ321198. A 19th-century building in the garden of a shop at 295 Junction Road. c.30ft (9·1m) × 14ft (4·3m) with a steep tiled roof it is in good condition and used as a store. The front half is open and the bakehouse occupied the back half, with the fire chamber at floor level and the oven above, reaching about halfway up the building. An iron plate on the oven is marked 'Patching & Son, Builders, Brighton' but no date is given. It was in use up till c.1960.

Keymer Brick & Tile Works, TQ323193. This extensive site containing several ranges of kilns besides beehive kilns was part of the main industry which resulted in the growth of the town. The nearby 19th-century workers' cottages may well have been

56 Bucks Green: bridge over R. Arun on disused Horsham–Guildford line; note iron girder above brick arch

associated with the works.

BURPHAM

Water pump, TQ042088. This small cast-iron pump and horse basket below a cottage window stand near one another beside the road running NE from the village.

BURY

Toll house, TQ010154. It is known that there was originally a toll house at this point, on B2138, and it is probably the present antique shop there, a small rectangular building of brick and stone with a tiled roof.

CHICHESTER

Warehouses, SU803046. A fine range of brick-built granaries on the E side of Boffins Lane. Dating from c.1870,

part of them has been converted to offices.

CLAPHAM

Toll house, TQ101075. Long Furlong Toll House, on A280 between Findon and Clapham, is a strange-looking castellated building, dating from 1820. The façade has a recess for the toll board which gave the charges (*Plate 57*).

CLAYTON

Railway tunnel, TQ298141. This 2259yd (2·1km) long tunnel on the London–Brighton line was opened in 1841 and was originally gas-lit. The strange castellated N portal can be easily seen from A273 with a cottage, still inhabited, in the centre behind the battlements, which is strangely out of keeping with the rest of the structure.

57   Clapham: castellated toll house on Long Furlong

Although David Mocatta was the architect for the Brighton line there is no evidence that he was responsible for the ornamentation on the portal. Spoil heaps and brick ventilation shafts for the tunnel can be seen over Clayton Hill beside A273.

Windmill ('Jack'), TQ304134. The upper of the 2 mills plainly visible on the hill to the S of B2116 as one approaches from Ditchling. It is a tower mill, built in 1876, disused and without sweeps for at least 50 years. It is now part of a dwelling house. The base of another mill can be seen nearby.

Windmill ('Jill'), TQ303134. The lower of the 2 mills on the hill, it is a post mill; built originally in Dyke Rd, Brighton, in 1821 and moved to its present position c.1850 by teams of oxen. Four sweeps and some of the machinery remain. It is maintained by Cuckfield Division of Mid-Sussex DC and may be visited by appointment.

COCKING

Railway station, SU875176. On the disused Chichester–Midhurst line. Buildings converted to private dwelling with sympathetic addition of first floor above original single-storey station buildings, beside 2-storey station master's house. Platform remains as a terrace, and goods yard now a garden. Fine plaster designs in panels on S end of house (*Plate 58*). See also WEST DEAN (SU876130).

CRABTREE

Hammer pond, TQ229251. The large pond here, extending up 2 branches of the valley, supplied the power for Gosden Furnace. The wood on the W side is known as Minepits Wood, indicating a source of ore, but it is probable that this did not produce a significant amount as there was intense

58   Cocking: plaster decoration on old station building, now a private house

competition between this furnace and the one at Hawkins Pond for access to the ore deposits further N in the forest. The furnace was built in 1580. (See ST LEONARD'S FOREST.)

CRAWLEY

Lowfield Heath Mill, TQ270399. This old post mill stands *c.*200yd (183m) W of A23, just by the roundabout at the S end of Gatwick Airport. Though originally in Surrey it is now in West Sussex. It is reported to have been transferred here from Hookwood in 1870. The brick roundhouse is roofless and the sweeps are missing; the windshaft, brake wheel, tail wheel and 2 pairs of stones still remain. It is in private hands and the owners have done what they can to maintain it. It has an unusually tall body with a very high steeply pitched roof. Efforts are being made to preserve and restore the mill.

CRAWLEY DOWN

Railway station, TQ324368. Rowfant Station, on the road from Crawley Down to Three Bridges, is the only remaining roadside station on the LB & SCR branch from Three Bridges to East Grinstead. Built in 1855, it is an attractive building with Gothic windows and steeply pitched roofs. It originally served Rowfant House, *c.*¼ mile (400m) NE of the station at TQ325372 and is now a private dwelling house, the railway having been closed in 1967.

CUCKFIELD

Watermill, TQ297236. Highbridge Mill, dating from the 18th century, is an old brick building with a gambrel roof, in fair condition. The iron overshot is usable and is being restored. The top part is now a dwelling house but the machinery remains; a wooden wallower and spur wheel, with 2 pairs of stones.

DUNCTON

Lime kiln, SU961163. Dating from about the middle of the 19th century this brick and flint structure contains 3 kilns side by side (*Plate 59*). It is on a public bridle path, *c.*300yd (274m) from A285 at the foot of Duncton Hill, and inset in a steep chalk hillside on the S side of the path. There are double brick and flint arches to the kilns with the grates set well back, the central one being the larger; two of the brick charging chambers are still open, about 25ft (7·6m) deep, tapering from 10ft (3m) diameter at the top to 7ft (2·1m) at the base. Generally in good condition though some of the upper brickwork is defective.

Watermill, SU964166. A 19th-century mill, now disused. The iron overshot wheel, some of the wooden machinery and 3 pairs of stones survive. The Southern Water Authority lease the mill pond for fish farming. The mill also drove a pump at one time.

EASEBOURNE

Bridge, SU896226. At the entrance to Cowdray Park on the S side of A272 there is a curious structure, rather like a lych-gate, which was a cattle grid, the adjacent gates, now removed, being opened for horse traffic. Although not used by wheeled traffic since 1939 the old notice boards still remain.

EAST GRINSTEAD

Imberhorne Viaduct, TQ383378. A 9-arched railway viaduct, of red-brick construction, on the East Grinstead–Lewes line (the Bluebell line). Opened in 1882 it was closed in 1958, but the

59 Duncton: lime kiln

track over it is still used as a reversing siding.

Watermill, TQ392368. An 18th/19th-century brick and timber building, now converted to a dwelling house, and gutted internally.

For milestones in this area of West Sussex on A22 (City of London–East Grinstead Turnpike Trust) refer to EAST SUSSEX, A22 MILESTONES. They are of the 'Bow Bells' type.

EAST MARDEN

Well, SU807146. The village well is on a triangle of grass opposite the church. An octagonal thatched roof supported on small tree trunks covers the winding gear, the operating handle of which is made from an old cartwheel hub with 4 spokes and a square rim. There is a single iron reduction gear, with a wooden brake on the windlass shaft, and a double-conical bucket with a narrow top.

EAST WITTERING

Windmill, SZ796972. A ruinous brick tower mill without cap or sweeps, now used as a store. It ceased working in 1890 but some of the wooden machinery is still left.

FITTLEWORTH

Watermill, TQ009184. The mill stands on the Western Rother, c.½ mile (800m) S of the village on B2138. A tall, ivy-clad, stone building in the garden of the former mill house; the iron waterwheel still remains, but the buckets have gone.

FORD

Disused airfield, SU989029. Opened at the start of 1918 as a training depot for the RFC it was known as Ford

Junction, or Yapton Airfield. In mid 1918 it was transferred to the US Army. In the 1939–45 war it was used as fighter station by the RAF, and subsequently by the Royal Navy. Three hangars still survive, 170ft (51·8m) × 100ft (30·5m) with timber bowstring roof trusses (Belfast trusses) supported on brick pillars. There are also the walls of a larger hangar, 380ft (115·8m) × 75ft (22·9m), probably dating from the time of use by the US Navy. Now mainly an industrial estate.

FUNTINGTON

Watermill, SU808074. West Ashling Mill, a 19th-century brick building in fair condition with the watermill at the W end of the building. An Armfield turbine has been installed to drive 3 pairs of stones. At the E end of the building the brick piers supporting a former hollow-post windmill still survive.

GAY STREET

Barn, TQ078203. At Lower Mill Farm, between Pulborough and Gay Street. A 3-bay 18th-century barn, timber-framed, with king posts and a corrugated-iron roof. The walls rest on brick and stone sills. In fairly good condition and in use until 1968.

HALNAKER

Windmill, SU920096. On top of Halnaker Hill. N of A285, c.1¼ miles (2km) NE of the village. A squat brick tower mill, with ogee cap and 4 sweeps, built c.1750 and restored externally as a landmark in 1934. The mill is an empty shell with dummy cap and common sails.

HANDCROSS

Hammer pond, TQ274294. In

Nymans Gardens (National Trust). A large pond, now a well-stocked lake, with the dam at the S end; in good condition with a well-built stepped stone spillway. The furnace was at the E end below the dam with the wheel pit probably just E of it. The public footpath to the site passes 2 small pen ponds.

HARDHAM

Canal tunnel, TQ032175–033171. Built in 1790 as part of the Arun Navigation, this 375yd (343m) long tunnel bypassed a 3-mile (4·83km) twisting loop of the R. Arun; it was blocked by the LB & SCR in 1898. The N portal, where there is water in the canal, is the better preserved, though the S portal is easier of access, but blocked. The dry and overgrown canal bed can be followed S from here till it joins the river just below Coldwaltham Lock at TQ023155.

HIGH SALVINGTON

Windmill, TQ122067. About .600yd (549m) W of A24 just N of Worthing. A post mill with round house, dating from c.1700, it has been well maintained and is being restored to working order. It is complete with 4 sweeps, all internal machinery, 2 pairs of stones, and a wire machine. The tail wheel is of the compass-arm type, the only one left in Sussex.

HORSHAM

Post box, TQ172304. A hinged wooden panel in the entrance to Pump Alley is an old letter box of the 'window' type dating from 1830. It is labelled 'Ye Olde Horsham Post Box'.
Tannery, TQ171302. This site, known as the Upper Tanyard, was one of 4 sites existing in Horsham in the 19th century. An iron-framed building with timber infilling, an unusual method of construction, it now forms part of a W Sussex CC depot.
Watermill, TQ169303. The Town Mill is a fine 3-storey building with 4 cast-iron columns from floor to roof in the centre. At the N end is a bypass sluice and wheel-pit for a breast-shot wheel, c.10ft (3m) in diameter, now removed though the control gear for the sluice still remains. In the centre, below floor level is a fine overshot wheel, c.10ft (3m) in diameter × 7ft (2·1m) wide, in very good condition. The breast-shot wheel was fed by an open tunnel from the mill pond, now silted up, but the overshot wheel was fed by an underground culvert beneath the mill yard. The cast-iron hursting, marked 'W.C. Cooper, Millwright, Henfield, 1867', for 3 pairs of stones with provision for a 4th, remains; these were driven via a layshaft from the overshot wheel and later, by belt-drive to the layshaft, from a steam engine, of which the foundations remain. Two further pairs of stones may have been driven from the breast-shot wheel, but no trace of the drive is left. The building may be converted to a dwelling house in the future. No stones are left and no machinery, only the large overshot wheel; the breast-shot wheel was a flood wheel.

HORSTED KEYNES

Railway station, TQ372292. The northern terminus, and carriage sheds, of the Bluebell Railway, the track ends c.500yd (457m) to the N but it is hoped it may be possible to restore the line N to East Grinstead. The station buildings have been very well restored and house a small collection of railway relics (see E. SUSSEX, SHEFFIELD PARK).
Smithy, TQ384282. A small single-storey building of brick on sandstone,

used as a private store and workshop since 1969.

Watermill, TQ380287. An 18th-century, 3-storey brick and timber building with tiled roof, in fairly good repair. An 18ft- (5·5m)-diameter over-shot wooden wheel, with iron machinery driving 2 pairs of stones and a saw. The present owner is preserving the mill and hopes to restore what is possibly the oldest watermill in Sussex.

Wheelwright's shop, TQ384281. A 19-century, 2-storey brick and corrugated iron building with a tiled roof. Remains of a small forge inside. Originally part of the Albion Iron Works, used for cart and waggon repairs and retyring. The smithy at TQ384282 was probably also a part of the works.

HOUGHTON

Toll house, TQ023118. At Houghton Bridge, on B2139, the Storrington–Balls Hut turnpike. Built in 1813 it is a single-storey flint and brick building with a small porch, but many additions have since been made to it.

HUNSTON

Canal bridge, SU860021. Almost the only visible remains of the Hundred of Manhood & Selsey Tramway, opened in 1897 and closed in 1935, which ran from Chichester to Selsey. The concrete abutments of the swing bridge on which the line crossed the Portsmouth and Arundel Canal are all that is left. They may be reached by walking down the canal towpath from Hunston.

Road bridge, SU864023. Poyntz Bridge crosses the Chichester Canal immediately N of its junction with the Portsmouth & Arundel Canal. Iron sections of the bridge, bearing the name and the date 1820, still remain in position. It is hoped that it will be possible to preserve this early canal drawbridge.

HURSTPIERPOINT

Watermill, TQ293180. Ruckford Mill near the headwaters of the R. Arun, c.1 mile (1·6km) W of A273 is a brick and timber building in good condition, converted into a dwelling house. The internal gearing still remains.

IFIELD

Watermill, TQ245364. A fine 19th-century, 4-storey brick and timber building with lucam, it has been very well restored by a local volunteer group for use by Crawley DC as an amenity and exhibition centre. The iron overshot wheel, and wheel-pit have been rebuilt, and the iron pen-trough, hursting, pit-wheel, wallower and spur-wheel from Hammonds Mill, now demolished, have been installed to replace the missing machinery. Some equipment from Balcombe Mill, which will be submerged in a new reservoir, has been salvaged and may also be installed at Ifield. A corn mill is known to have been on this site since the 16th century, probably on the site of an earlier water-powered forge. It was rebuilt in 1683 (a tablet on the wall records the names of Thomas and Mary Middleton) and was rebuilt again in 1817 but was out of use by the 1930s.

KEYMER

Windmill, TQ321162. This 18th-century post mill (Oldlands Mill) with octagonal brick round-house stands in the garden of a private house and is owned by the Sussex Archaeological Society. Most of the machinery is present, though 2 sweeps are missing, but the body is in a partially collapsed condition. The remaining sweeps have patent sails with elliptical springs. Plans are in hand to save the structure from further deterioration, and perhaps ultimately to restore the mill to working order. Approach is by a private road turning E off the Keymer–Burgess Hill road, at a sharp corner S of Ockley Manor.

LAVANT

Railway station, SU856086. On the disused Chichester–Midhurst line. On N side of A286 beside road bridge over the railway. The station lies in a deep cutting with the station master's house, now a private dwelling, built on top of the station buildings. Platform, canopy and buildings remain but derelict. Good cast-iron columns supporting the canopy. Tracks lifted. Old footbridge S of roadbridge remains.

LINDFIELD

Old brewery, TQ346254. The remains of the brewery lie behind Durrant's grocery, whose family also owned the Stand Up Inn next door. A brick chimney and some sheds alongside formed part of the brewery.

Horse-gin, TQ347254. At the Stand Up Inn opposite the old toll house is a horse-gin house comprising an octagonal slated roof supported on wooden pillars. The brick-paved track for the horse still remains in position.

Horse-gin, TQ349259. At Old Place the iron cage of the horse-gin stands above the well and 2 pumps at the bottom of the well are operated by a crankshaft driven by a bevel gear-wheel on the vertical shaft. Though on private ground the machine can be seen from the lane behind the church (*Plate 60*).

Toll house, TQ347254. A late medieval

60 Lindfield: horse-gin mounted above well

timber-framed cottage with brick in-fill, now 58 High Street, was used as a toll house right up to 1884 when the gates were removed and publicly burned. The date 1603 is on the front.
Watermill, TQ377258. Cockhaise Mill, *c.*200yd (183m) W of Freshfield Halt on the Bluebell Railway, is a 18th/19th-century brick and timber building in good condition and now a dwelling house. All machinery has gone except for the framing of the hursting and the 12ft- (3.7m)-diameter iron overshot wheel, which dates from 1883.
Watermill, TQ354262. Deans Mill, on the R. Ouse, on the W side of B2028 near Lindfield Bridge, was the last regularly working watermill in Sussex, producing stone-ground flour. A tall, white, brick and timber building, it dates from 1881 and has an iron breast-shot wheel driving 4 pairs of stones and flour-dressing machines. An earlier flour mill and a paper mill

on the same site were destroyed by fire. Unfortunately it ceased working in 1977 and is now becoming derelict.

LITTLEHAMPTON

Brewery, TQ028021. George Constable's brewery in East Street, a yellow-brick building with a ventilator on top, is now a bottling plant. It dates from *c.*1860.
Malt house, TQ028021. In East Street and visible from the car park in Duke Street, this is a typical 19th-century kiln, square, cement-rendered, with a slate roof.
Swing bridge, TQ022022. This bridge, opened in 1908 to replace a ferry, originally carried A259 over the R. Arun, but is now only a footbridge having been superseded by the modern road bridge a short distance upstream (*Plate 61*). It was originally operated manually, later by a diesel engine, from the operating cabin on top of the

61 Littlehampton: swing bridge

central structure, the drive being taken down by gearing and shafting to a toothed ring under the bridge, and also to the locking devices at both ends. It is unfortunately due for demolition as it is an obstruction to navigation.

Workshops, TQ022021–TQ023020. Several stores and workshops dating from the first half of the 19th century still remain along River Road, notably Duke & Ockenden's who are still in business as well-known makers of pumps and other machinery. Some of their old water pumps can still be seen at sites in Sussex, though now no longer in use.

LOXWOOD

Watermill, TQ046311. Brewhurst Mill, on a tributary of the R. Arun, lies close to the Wey & Arun Canal. A 19th-century timber building on a brick ground floor, it is in excellent condition. A cast-iron overshot wheel and the iron internal machinery survive, though the drive is now from a modern oil engine. There is iron breast-shot flood wheel on the N side.

LYMINSTER

Old railway station, TQ028039. The former Littlehampton and Arundel Station where A284 crosses the railway. The goods shed still survives but all the other buildings have recently been demolished.

MIDHURST

Toll house, SU875218. On A272 c.1½ miles (2·4km) W of Midhurst; the road was turnpiked c.1825. The part of the house that is the original toll house is a plain rectangle with a projecting porch.
Watermill, SU889220. On the Western Rother where A286 crosses it between Midhurst and Easebourne, North Mill

was formerly a large corn mill for the Cowdray Estate, having 2 breast-shot wheels and 2 sets of machinery. The stone building has been completely gutted inside and converted to private dwellings.

MILLAND MARSH

Horse-gin, SU862262. All that is left of a small brickyard at Redford on the E side of the Midhurst–Liphook road just N of Woolbeding Common is a horse-gin house; the horse-gin possibly drove the pug-mill. It is hexagonal, of brick and local stone, with a tiled roof and a brick floor. It is in fair condition and is used as a store for agricultural machinery.

NORTHCHAPEL

Toll house, SU953296. On A283 just N of the village green. A single-storey, red-brick building of a shallow T-shape, set at right angles to the road. It dates from c.1757.

NORTH HEATH

Lock, TQ038214. Pallingham Lock on the Arun Navigation is a double lock where the canal joins the river, which is tidal up to this point. Derelict, it is now in the garden of the modernized lock cottage which is a private dwelling. A little way N of the lock a public footpath crosses the canal by the original masonry bridge, which has now been preserved by adding a thin reinforced-concrete skin above and below it (*Plate 62*), beside Pallingham Quay at TQ038216. Pallingham Dock is immediately S of this at TQ038215. The whole area is much overgrown and difficult of access.

NURSTEAD

Watermill, SU765210. About 250yd

(229m) E of B2146 an 18th-century building with a wooden overshot wheel and 19th-century iron machinery, but no stones. It was used until the 1960s to raise water to the mill house alongside. It is in fair condition and cared for.

NUTBOURNE

Windmill, TQ078179. All that is left of this brick tower mill is the tower, with no cap and with the remains of the machinery fallen across the tower.

NYETIMBER

Windmill, SZ892988. On W side of a road from North Mundham to Pagham, all that is left of this 19th-century tower mill is an overgrown tower without cap, with the machinery just visible at the top. The cap was destroyed by fire. The windshaft and arms of the brake-wheel still remain.

NYEWOOD

Rogate Railway Station, SU803219. On the disused Pulborough–Petersfield line. A plain station building, stuccoed, now used as a factory.

OREHAM COMMON

Watermill, TQ217317. About 1½ miles (2·4km) S of Henfield on A2037, Woods Mill is the headquarters of the Sussex Trust for Nature Conservation. The mill, on a tributary of the Adur, is an 18th-century, 4-storey stone and brick building with timber-framed upper floors. The iron launder for the 9ft- (2·7m)-diameter iron wheel bears the name Neal & Cooper, Henfield, and the date 1854. The internal machinery is modern and was reconstructed a few years ago to demonstrate the working of a typical watermill. Open May to September except Mondays.

62   North Heath: Pallingham Bridge on Wey & Arun Canal

PARTRIDGE GREEN

Water tower, TQ196193. An old brick water tower stands in a field on the S side of B2116 $c.\frac{1}{2}$ mile (800m) E of its junction with B2135, and just before the 30mph sign.

PATCHING

Horse-gin, TQ087066. In a field E of the churchyard, from which it is visible, though now buried in brambles, this mid 19th-century horse-gin drove a 3-throw pump lifting water from a 150ft- (46m)-deep well. With its circular concrete track for the horse it is a good example of this type of installation.

PETWORTH

Ice-house, SU976222. This ice-house, situated on the Petworth Estate, is certainly the finest in Sussex. It comprises 3 very large chambers, $c.$30ft

(9·1m) deep and lies beneath the old fire-engine house.

Iron artifacts, SU976219. At Petworth House (National Trust) there is a good collection of iron fire-backs in one of the corridors.

Lamp standard, SU977217. An extraordinary cast-iron erection at the junction of North Street and East Street. It was designed by Sir Charles Barry in 1851.

Railway station, SU970191. Just E of the overbridge on A285 S of Coultershaw Bridge. A fine wooden station building, typical of the LB & SCR construction for country stations, it lies on the abandoned Pulborough–Midhurst line. Though derelict the building is not in too bad a condition and has 3 good brick chimney stacks (*Plate 63*). It is threatened by development and it is hoped it may be possible to save it, either on site or by dismantling and re-erection at a suitable site elsewhere.

63 Petworth: disused railway station

Water-pumping station, SU972194. Situated just beside Coultershaw Bridge, where A285 crosses the Western Rother, this 18th-century water-driven pumping station lay beneath the floor of the now vanished Coultershaw Mill. Installed by Lord Egremont in 1782, it replaced an earlier water supply system to the town said to have been constructed *c.*1500 by the Rev. John Edwards, Rector of Petworth 1496–1531, thus making Petworth possibly the first town in England to have a pumped water supply. The installation consists of a 11·5ft-(3·5m)-diameter breastshot wheel, 4ft 6in (1·4m) wide, with wooden paddles and sole-boards and cast-iron arms and rim. It is mounted on a massive iron shaft, 7in (178mm) in diameter, which is coupled to a 5in- (127mm)-diameter iron 3-throw crankshaft, the connecting rods from which are attached to 3 wooden beams *c.*15ft (4·6m) long, pivoted at one end. To the opposite ends are attached the pump rods, operating in a 6in- (152mm)-diameter triple-barrelled, open-topped iron pump body (*Plate 64*). Water was delivered from this, via a 3in- (76mm)-diameter cast-iron pipe nearly 1½ miles (2·4km) long to a 23,000-gallon (104,558 litre) reservoir on Lawn Hill in Petworth Park, and to a large stone cistern in Grove Street, Petworth. The former supplied all the needs of Petworth House and grounds, and the latter supplied the town. The pump operated regularly until 1960, supplying the gardens and stables at Petworth, and is currently being restored to working order by the Sussex Industrial Archaeology Society, who hope to have it working again by the end of 1977.

PORTSLADE-BY-SEA

Electricity generating station, TQ256042. Brighton 'A' Generating Station was built by Brighton Corporation between 1904 and 1906 superseding an earlier one at Gloucester Road built in 1882, making Brighton one of the first towns in Britain to have a public electricity supply. The 'A' Station operated for nearly 70 years but is now closed down and may be demolished in the near future. It contained a 50MW Ljungström turbo-alternator, the largest of this type manufactured in Britain.

POYNINGS

Donkey wheel, TQ273114. Saddlescombe donkey wheel raised water from a well, *c.*175ft (53m) deep, in wooden buckets which were tipped into lead-lined cisterns. The wooden wheel, dating from the 18th/19th centuries has tangential spokes which are fitted in opposite directions on each side; 14ft (4·3m) diameter × 3ft 9in (1·1m) wide it needed 28 turns to raise the bucket. It is housed in a small timber building, open on the E side, and well maintained by Brighton Corporation, the owners. It was in use until *c.*1910, worked by a donkey or 2 men (*Plate 65*).

PULBOROUGH

Sand mine, TQ063193. A series of galleries, now much overgrown, slope gently down into the hillside beside the road from Marehill to Broomershill. Sand was extracted on the pillar-and-stall method as and when it was needed.

RACKHAM

Watermill, TQ046142. A small 19th-century watermill on the Parham Estate, on the edge of Amberley Wild Brooks. It has been kept in good condition, though not in working order.

64   Petworth: water pumps at Coultershaw Bridge; the pump rods are behind the connecting rods from the crankshaft

Iron overshot wheel and mainly wooden machinery with 2 pairs of stones.

ST LEONARD'S FOREST

Hammer ponds. Among the few visible remains of the Wealden iron industry are 2 fine hammer ponds, both lying just N of the road from Horsham to Slaugham, Hawkins Pond at TQ216292 and Hammer Pond at TQ219289. The former supplied a furnace and a forge, and the latter a forge only. All the forges were built about the mid 16th century and the furnace in 1584, but the furnace was shut down c.1615 and the forges in 1644. In each case the wheel-pits were probably at the E end of the dam where the present overflow sluice is sited. At Hawkins Pond the foundations and some timber remains of buildings can be seen below the dam c.30yd (27·4m) W of the overflow sluice. The ore for the furnace probably came from the

neighbourhood of Colgate (TQ231328) in the N part of the forest, where there are numerous pits in the beech woods (see also CRABTREE TQ229251 and SLAUGHAM TQ249280).

SAYERS COMMON

Watermill, TQ274190. Cobb's Mill, on the upper reaches of the R. Adur, is on a side road c.1½ miles (2·4km) N of Hurstpierpoint. It is a 19th-century brick and timber building, attached to a private house, and was in use up to 1966. The building and machinery have been kept in very good condition by the owner, though the external 11ft-(3·3m)-diameter iron overshot wheel needs new buckets (*Plate 66*). All internal machinery is present, including 2 fine cleaning and dressing machines. Four pairs of stones in line are driven from a layshaft which is parallel to the wheel shaft. An auxiliary drive from a Tangye gas engine is connected

65   Poynings: Saddlescombe donkey wheel

66　Sayers Common: Cobb's Mill under flood conditions

to the middle of the layshaft by a movable pinion; the gas-production plant is still in existence. The owner is anxious to preserve this most interesting and unusual installation.

SELSEY

Medmerry Windmill, sz844934. A brick tower mill near the seashore. Built c.1829 it has been privately restored externally as a landmark and stands in a caravan park. There are 4 dummy sweeps and the brake-wheel and wallower still remain.

SHARPTHORNE

Tanyard, TQ375308. On the E side of the Sharpthorne–Horsted Keynes road, c.1 mile (1·6km) S of Sharpthorne. An interesting little museum of tanning and leather preparation attached to a lovely private house. The building is medieval with 16th- and 17th-century additions and the site of the tanning pit can be seen together with the arrangements for supplying water to it. Open May to September 2 to 5 pm. Parties by appointment.

SHIPLEY

Hammer pond, TQ157211. The hammer pond of Knepp Furnace c.½ mile (800m) W of A24 is one of the largest pieces of water in Sussex. The furnace was worked from 1568 to 1604.
Road gate, TQ151229. Shipley Gate is an odd survival from the turnpike days. A small section of road, just S of the cross-roads where B224 crosses A272, is barred by a road gate with a pedestrian wicket and the road S makes a detour round it. The site of the toll house is now occupied by a Victorian mansion.
Windmill, TQ143219. Just W of the village stands the largest smock mill in

Sussex (*Plate 67*). Built in 1879 it worked until 1926 and was restored to full working order in 1958 as a memorial to Hilaire Belloc who owned the mill from 1906 until his death; it now belongs to one of his daughters. It is of the usual octagonal shape with fantail, standing on a 2-storey octagonal brick base, with clasp-arm brakewheel, iron wallower and 3 pairs of stones, underdriven from an iron spurwheel. Open first Saturday and Sunday of each month, May to September, 2.30 to 5.45 pm. Corn is ground on some weekends.

SHOREHAM-BY-SEA

Harbour buildings, TQ235049. The single-storey brick Custom House opposite the harbour entrance, built 1886 and in use until 1969, is now the local Scout HQ. Just to the E of it is the old lighthouse, a stone tower with a ring base of stone and a modern lantern; the date 1846 is painted over the doorway. At TQ242049 is the original lock at the entrance to the 3000yd (2·7km) ship canal to the Aldrington Basin, built in 1854. It was converted to a dry dock in 1934 when the first of the modern locks was built on the S side, which has electrically operated gates. The latest lock, built in 1950, has hydraulically operated gates. At TQ265048, on the N side of Aldrington Basin, under the cliff, are a few single-storey brick and flint sheds, with hipped roofs, probably dating from 1854 when the basin was built. They are all that is left of a continuous row of 24 sheds, probably used for storage of carts and possibly stabling of horses. (Although the E end of Aldrington Basin is actually in East Sussex, it is treated here under West Sussex, as it is part of Shoreham Harbour.)
Marlipins Museum, TQ215050. On

67 Shipley: smock mill

the N side of Shoreham High Street. The building dates from the 12th to 14th centuries and is owned by the Sussex Archaeological Society. There are pictures of the old railway and the Brighton–Shoreham Tramway and old maps of Shoreham Harbour. It also houses an interesting collection of ship models and pictures, and has a number of cast-iron fire-backs, fire-dogs, a cannon and other iron artifacts.

Old fort, TQ233045. At the extreme E end of Shoreham Beach on the W side of the harbour entrance. The remains of the fort, built in 1857, consist of an inner wall built in 2 straight lines meeting at an angle, with emplacements for 6 guns pointing seawards, and an outer wall set in a ditch with 3 projections to allow enfilading fire along the straight stretches of wall. The pivots and circular arcs of rail for the gun tails still remain together with 3 recesses for shells and an underground magazine. The barracks have gone but their foundations can still be traced.

Toll bridge, TQ207059. Old Shoreham Bridge, built in 1781 was the original road crossing of the R. Adur, c.¼ mile (400m) below the present viaduct on A27. A timber bridge, with 2 passing places in the middle, it has been many times rebuilt but always to the original pattern (*Plate 68*). Tolls were collected here at least up to the 1930s, but it is now free and used only as a footbridge. A very interesting survival of an early type of construction.

Toll house, TQ213051. Just E of Norfolk Bridge, where A259 crosses the R. Adur is a flat-roofed, single-storey cottage in the classical style with a moulded cornice. It dates from 1833 and is contemporary with the first Norfolk Bridge, an elegant suspension one built by W. Tierney Clark, and similar to his bridge over the Thames at Marlow. It was replaced by the present bridge in 1922.

68   Shoreham-by-Sea: old toll bridge

SINGLETON

Open air museum, SU875129. The Weald & Downland Open Air Museum, just S of Singleton on the Goodwood road is a museum of old buildings which have been saved from demolition and re-erected on a part of the West Dean Estate. Its industrial exhibits include the 18th-century Lurgashall Watermill, removed from its original site at SU940259, a blacksmith's shop, wheelwright's shop, horse-gin and toll cottage. There is also a good farm exhibition and a fine barn and granaries. Open Easter to October, every day except Mondays. During October it may only be open 2 or 3 days in the week.

SLAUGHAM

Hammer pond, TQ249280. A large furnace pond just W of the crossroads at Slaugham Common on the N side of the road. The furnace was started in 1574 and closed down c.1653. The ore for this furnace probably came from the N part of the forest. There is a feeder pond just N of the main pond (see ST LEONARD'S FOREST). **Watermill,** TQ258277. The shell of a small 19th-century building with no machinery left. In the bottom is an old turbine which once drove a dynamo for generating electricity.

SOMERLEY

Windmill, SZ817984. On E side of B2198, Earnley Mill is an interesting 18th-century smock mill with a tarred body on a brick base, and an ogee cap. Of 3 floors, nearly all its mainly wooden machinery is intact. An iron windshaft and wallower, but wooden brakewheel, upright shaft and spur-wheel. It has been preserved by its owner who is now restoring it.

SOUTH HARTING

Water-pumping station, SU785191. A small building on the E side of B2146, at the entrance to the village from the S once housed a waterwheel-driven pump that delivered water from a 250ft- (76m)- deep well to the house at Uppark, c.1 mile (1·6km) to the S and c.350ft (107m) higher. The overshot waterwheel has gone, though the launder remains inside the house together with the layshaft and gearwheel (minus wooden teeth) that once drove the pump. The building is on the Uppark Estate, which is National Trust property. The mill pond is dry and overgrown.

SOUTHBOURNE

Disused airfield, SU768063. A small industrial estate occupies the site of this airfield just over ½ mile (800m) N of A27; built in 1918 for the US Navy, it was never occupied by them. Some of its buildings are now used for industrial purposes.

SOUTHWATER

Brickworks, TQ158260. These extensive works, on the E side of A24 just N of its junction with B2224 once belonged to the Sussex & Dorking United Brick Co. The old clay pit is now filled with water.

STEYNING

Watermill, TQ172115. Court Mill, on the NW edge of the town just W of A283 is now part of a Victorian private dwelling. However, the brick and timber mill still retains its character with gambrel roof and lucam, composite overshot wheel and some machinery.

STOPHAM

Road bridge, TQ030184. This stone bridge, built in 1423, carries A283 over the R. Arun. Very narrow, with safety bays above the piers, it has one-way traffic controlled by lights. The 6 side arches are original, but the centre arch was enlarged in 1822.

STORRINGTON

Tannery, TQ089142. On the S side of A283 near the centre of the town the horse-gin house is all that is left of the old tannery. It is an octagonal building made of split logs placed vertically and is now used as a store.

Toll house, TQ071135. A single-storey brick and flint cottage with slate roof on S side of B2139 at a sharp bend. The road was turnpiked in 1812 and the spot is still marked 'Paygate' on the 2½in (1:25,000) OS map.

Windmill shaft, TQ098142. All that is left of Sullington Mill that once stood on a slight hill on Sullington Warren and was burnt down in 1911. The cast-iron shaft has a poll-end and sockets for a clasp-arm brake-wheel but no provision for a tail-wheel. It lies behind some gorse bushes beside a seat, on the common on the N side of A283, which faces the site of the old mill.

TROTTON

Watermills, SU831222. Terwick Mills on the Western Rother are c.700yds (640m) SW of the village church. There are 2 mills, the older, dating from the 14th century, being timber built and tarred with 1 pair of stones, while the newer one, built in 1745, is of local stone and brick with 2 pairs of stones. The buildings are adjoining with the 2 water wheels between them, the older one being quite narrow with only one set of arms, while the newer one is of normal width; both are low breast-shot

wheels. Internally the older mill is nearly derelict but the newer one, converted to a private dwelling in 1973, still has the machinery intact and preserved for inspection. The mill ceased work in 1966 and the tail-race is much silted up.

TWINEHAM

Toll house, TQ268203. On the W side of A23 immediately S of the crossroads in Hickstead village. An old brick and timber cottage, once the Castle Inn toll house. An inserted window gives a view of traffic approaching from London.

WARNHAM

Brickworks, TQ171344. This old-established brickworks, originally the Sussex Brick Co, then Sussex & Dorking United, and now part of the Redland Brick Co, lies just to the E of the railway, N of Warnham Station. A terrace of tile-hung and brick cottages beside Warnham Station may well be workers' cottages built by the company.

Watermill, TQ168323. On A24 c.300yd (274m) SE of the roundabout at the N end of the Horsham bypass, this red-brick building with Horsham stone roof is now sadly decayed. The composite overshot wheel, though covered, is in poor condition; it drove 3 pairs of stones through mainly iron machinery. The very large mill pond was probably originally made for Warnham Furnace, c.1600.

WASHINGTON

Lime kilns, TQ120123. On the old road S from the village a cart track leads off to the E after c.¼ mile (400m); this runs uphill and passes the mouth of the kilns which are rather buried in the undergrowth. Dating from the 19th century, there are 3 kilns, 2 in fair condition and 1 smaller one in rather poor condition. They are c.20ft (6m) high, faced with brick and chalk blocks with loading bays in front; the charging chambers are now filled with debris. At this spot 3 different ages of road run side-by-side; the cart track is almost certainly part of the old road from Worthing to the Weald before the turnpike, just below and W of it and which it joins further on, was made; while further to the W and lower still is the modern A24 trunk road by-passing the village.

Windmill, TQ128132. On Rock Common, N of A283 and W of A24 near a minor road joining the 2 roads. A smock mill without sweeps, built c.1819 and converted to a dwelling house in 1919.

WEST CHILTINGTON

Old engines, TQ085182. Mr Charles Hudson has assembled an interesting collection of old oil and gas engines, all of which have been restored to working order and can be run.

Windmill, TQ085181. On a road fork c.700yd (640m) SW of the cross-roads in centre of village. This smock mill was built c.1838 and the brick base incorporated into a private dwelling house in 1922. It still has the gallery and 2 sweeps but no fantail.

WEST DEAN

Ice-house, SU862119. This very impressive ice-house on the West Dean Estate has its own paved loading bay.

Singleton Railway Station, SU867130. On the disused Chichester–Midhurst line. At end of a tree-lined drive to private grounds on N side of A286. Platform and station buildings at upper level above station master's house, which has been converted to provide a wine press for adjacent vineyard. Cast-iron columns to canopy on entrance side preserved with a transparent roof to protect plaster designs in panels on walls, which also contain date '1880' and name 'L.B. & S.C.R.' (see also COCKING (SU875176)).

WEST HOATHLY

Iron grave slabs, TQ363326. Two cast-iron grave slabs on the wall of S aisle commemorate 2 Richard Infelds, dated 1619 and 1624. On N wall of chancel is a cast-iron slab with indecipherable inscription, but a brass plate alongside gives the details; it commemorates a daughter of Richard Infeld and is dated 1635. The Infelds were ironmasters who built Gravetye Manor. In the churchyard are several 19th-century, cast-iron monuments, mostly of a fairly standard pattern, but one unusual one is in the form of an iron plate c.5ft (1·5m) long × c.1ft (30cm) high. In the NW corner of the church, inside, are the iron works of an old turret clock believed to date from 1410–22, which originally had a foliot escapement, replaced by a pendulum c.1700. The clock was removed from the tower in 1965.

WISBOROUGH GREEN

Aquaduct, TQ058246. Orfold Aquaduct carries the Arun Navigation over the R. Arun. Of brick construction with 3 arches, the retaining wall on the SE side is missing, and the structure acts as a weir on the Arun. Immediately S of the aquaduct the walls of Orfold Lock (or Lordings Lock) on the Arun are well preserved. Further S there were flood gates on the river, under a farm bridge. This section of the Arun Navigation is dry and much overgrown. The aquaduct may be reached by a track from Orfold Farm and then W along the canal bank or by the bridleway S from Wisborough Green and then E along the canal bank. By either route the access is difficult.

Wharf and Warehouse, TQ069258. Where A272 crosses the R. Arun at Newbridge there is an old wharf and warehouse S of the bridge on the W bank of the canal. Built in 1839 they are in good repair and used as farm buildings. The canal is in water here but the bridge under A272 is blocked.

WOODGATE

Old railway station, SU939043. The original LB & SCR station for Bognor before the present branch from Barn-

ham was built in 1864, it stands where A29 crosses the railway. The station building, single-storey, and the tiny crossing-keeper's cottage, both now private dwellings are in the red brick and flint style typical of the LB & SCR from 1845–7.

WORTHING

Museum, TQ148029. There are a few good railway engine and ship models; also a Victorian post box and a manual fire-engine of 1890.

Pier, TQ150023. The pier was built 1861–2 and has been recommended for listing as a Grade II structure. There are some pleasant old cast-iron lamp standards on the railings along its length.

Bibliography

Abbreviations: *SIH – Sussex Industrial History.*
   Arch. Cant. – Archaeologica Cantiana.

GENERAL

Aldsworth, F. *Archaeology in West Sussex – A Field Guide,* West Sussex County Council, 1977.

Bennett, C.E. 'The Watermills of Kent, East of the Medway', *Industrial Archaeology Review,* Vol. 1, No 3, Summer 1977, p 205.

Cossons, N. *The BP Book of Industrial Archaeology,* David & Charles, 1975.

Payne, G.A., *Surrey Industrial Archaeology,* Phillimore, 1977. Mills.

Wilson, G. *The Old Telegraphs,* Phillimore, 1977.

Wooldridge, S.W. and Goldring, F. *The Weald,* Collins, 1953. *Archaeologica Cantiana,* Kent Archaeological Society, continuing. *Sussex Archaeological Collections,* Sussex Archaeological Society, continuing. *Sussex Industrial History,* Nos 1–6, Phillimore, Chichester, 1970–4 (No 4 was published as *Sussex Industrial Archaeology – A Field Guide,* 1972). *Sussex Industrial History,* No 7, Sussex Industrial Archaeology Society, 1977.

WEALDEN IRON INDUSTRY

Straker, E. *Wealden Iron,* Bell, 1931 (republished by The Library Association, 1967). *Wealden Iron,* Nos 1–10, Wealden Iron Research Group, 1969–76.

WEALDEN GLASS INDUSTRY

Kenyon, G.H. *The Glass Industry of the Weald,* Leicester University Press, 1967.

MILLS

Brunner, H. and Major, J.K. *Water Raising by Animal Power,* Offprint from *Industrial Archaeology,* Vol 9, No 2, May 1972, David & Charles.

Ferries, K.G. and Mason, M.T. *Windmills of Surrey and Inner London,* Skilton, 1967.

Henning, P. *Windmills in Sussex,* C.W. Daniel, London, 1936.

Hillier, J. *Old Surrey Watermills,* Skeffington, 1951.

Reynolds, J. *Windmills and Watermills,* Hugh Evelyn, London, 1970.

Smith, A.C. *Windmills in Surrey and Greater London – A contemporary Survey,* Stevenage Museum, 1976.

Syson, L. *British Watermills,* London, 1965.

Wailes, R. *The English Windmill,* Routledge and Kegan Paul, 1967.

—— *Windmills in England,* Architectural Press, 1948 (reprinted Skilton, 1975).

West, J. *The Windmills of Kent,* Skilton, 1974.

Percival, A. *The Faversham Gunpowder Industry,* published as Faversham Papers, No 4 by The Faversham Society.

RAILWAYS

Body, G. and Eastleigh, R.L. *Cliff Railways,* David & Charles, 1964.

Catt, A.R. *The East Kent Railway,* Oakwood, Lingfield, 1970.

Forwood, M. *The Elham Valley Railway*, Unwin, 1975.

Garrett, S.R. *The Kent & East Sussex Railway*, Oakwood, Lingfield, 1972.

Griffith, E. *The Selsey Tramways*, E.C. Griffith, 8 Mavins Road, Farnham, 1974.

Measom, G. *The Official Illustrated Guide to the South Eastern Railway and its Branches*, E & W Books (Publishers) Ltd., 1970. Facsimile reprint of the first edition of 1858. Communications.

Symes, R. and Cole, D. *Railway Architecture of the South East*, Osprey, Reading, 1972.

White, H.P. *Forgotten Railways – South East England*, David & Charles, 1976.

CANALS

Rolt, L.T.C. *Navigable Waterways*, Longmans, 1969.

Vine, P.A.L. *London's Lost Route to Basingstoke*, David & Charles, 1968.

—— *London's Lost Route to the Sea*, David & Charles, 1965.

—— *The Royal Military Canal*, David & Charles, 1972.

PORTS AND HARBOURS

Farrant, J.H. *Mid-Victorian Littlehampton, The Railway and the Cross-Channel Steamers*, published as Littlehampton Papers No 4 by Littlehampton UDC, 1972.

—— *The Harbours of Sussex*, J.H. Farrant, 12 Dudwell Road, Woodingdean, Brighton, 1976.

Glossary

BASCULE – The portion of a lifting bridge that hinges upwards.

BREAST-SHOT WHEEL – A water wheel where the water enters at about mid-height.

CROWNTREE – The main cross beam of a post mill which rotates on the top of the post and carries the body of the mill.

HAMMER POND – A pond supplying the water wheel which drives the trip hammer of a forge, or the bellows of a blast furnace.

LAUNDER – A trough, of wood or iron, carrying the water to the top of a water wheel.

LUCAM – The projecting structure on the top storey of a water mill, or warehouse, containing a hoist for raising grain, or goods, to the upper floors.

PEN POND – A small pond, often one of a series, constructed in the upper reaches of a valley, for storing water to be released later to feed the hammer pond (q.v.).

QUANT – The square shaft driving the upper millstone from above. This type of drive is common in windmills but met with occasionally in watermills.

TRASH RACK – An iron or wooden grid across the water course upstream from a watermill to prevent floating debris from entering the water wheel or turbine.

WALLOWER – A bevel pinion on the vertical shaft of a mill which meshes with, and is driven by, a larger bevel wheel on the horizontal shaft of the mill carrying the sails of a windmill or the water wheel of a watermill.

Index

This index is arranged by subjects to show the sites where material relative to a particular subject may be seen.
The different counties are indicated as follows:
K – Kent; S – Surrey; ES – East Sussex; WS – West Sussex.

Museums